"In the first place, we don't li.. ..
—Hannah Arendt, *We Refugees,* 1943

"The tragedy of modern man is not that he knows less
and less about the meaning of his own life,
but that it bothers him less and less."

—Vaclav Havel, Former President of Czechoslovakia,
Author of *Letters to Olga,* 1988

Praise for Miriam Hoffman
and *A Breed Apart*

"It's an honor to write of a member of the greatest generation. **A feisty little Jew . . .** Miriam has captured the pain inflicted by going through Polish discrimination, Nazi fratricide, the DP camps, the flame of Israel's ignition, and then the struggle to survive in still shaping America. **She's a survivor, who today can stand 10-feet tall by turning flesh into steel. I praise her!**"

—Ed Asner, Actor and Activist

"What a wonderful surprise! **I read *A Breed Apart* in one sitting,** impervious to dinner or anything else until I finished. **I was so moved** by Miriam's early childhood memories in the USSR during the war and her years at the Hindenburg Kaserne, delightfully enriched by her droll sense of humor and descriptions of friends, the community, and most of all, her remarkable and idiosyncratic parents who got her through historically dangerous times in their very different, but brave ways."

—Gail Merrifield Papp, surviving spouse of Joseph Papp
(American theatrical producer and supporter of Yiddish theatre)

"**Miriam Hoffman is the world's greatest living Yiddish author** and one of a handful of master Yiddish educators and scholars whose depth of knowledge, sharpness of intellect, and love of sharing with others combines with profoundly authentic Yiddish culture, humor, wit, and modes of thinking to make for a leading Yiddish phenomenon of our time. This book, in fact, is Miriam's personal story, an extraordinary true-life saga from Soviet Siberia through the little understood post-Holocaust DP camps to the status of the finest Yiddish educator Columbia University has had this century. **It is a story we should all come to read, appreciate, and love.**"

—Professor Dovid Katz, Vilnius Gediminas
Technical University, Lithuania

"**Miriam Hoffman has a unique sense of history and humanity.** She was born at a time when it was easier to perish than to survive, growing up amongst the horror and suffering. As a child, she experienced the journey of a refugee, through Soviet Russia, Poland, the DP Camps in Germany, and finally reaching the safety of America. Her creativity is saturated with the 'juices' of Yiddish life, wit, joy, and pain. Miriam never lacks for themes in her creative writing, as she always arrives at the inspired shores of humanity."

—Boris Sandler, Documentarian/Former Editor of the Yiddish Forward

"I knew Miriam Hoffman as a Columbia University professor and Yiddish playwright. What I didn't know before reading this remarkable memoir was the life she lived before coming to America: her birth in Siberia (where her father was imprisoned), her harrowing escape through post-War Eastern Europe, and her childhood in a displaced persons camp in Germany. **Professor Hoffman tells her compelling personal story within a broader historical context. Alive with anecdote, *A Breed Apart* is a tale of catastrophe, survival, cultural rebirth and hope.**"

—Aaron Lansky, Author of *Outwitting History: The Amazing Adventures of a Man Who Rescued a Million Yiddish Books*

"The author is the most engaging companion, taking us firmly and charmingly through the most harrowing of early conditions to climbing the rungs of the canonized American dream. In her spirited prose she **captures the universal nature of childhood: observant, reckless, guileless yet wily, and heroically able to cope with adversity.** Professor Hoffman, with her life's blood pumping courageously along from the slave labor camp under soviet rule to Israel's land of milk and honey to the urban sophistication of Manhattan, always tells a juicy anecdote that makes one simultaneously chuckle and feel touched. This book, with its illustrative photos of the author's buoyant and idiosyncratic family and its understanding of the journey from existence to survival to thriving, allows no room for drifting thoughts. **You are in the author's world until the last line.**"

—Julie Gilbert, novelist, biographer, playwright, teacher, The Writer's Academy, The Kravis Center for the Performing Arts

"**An exilic journey of epic proportions**, Professor Miriam Hoffman's memoir, *A Breed Apart,* insightfully describes the rich and multifaceted life of a major Jewish pedagogue, Yiddishist, writer, essayist, playwright, and public intellectual. Deeply rooted in Stalin's infamous Siberian Gulag and profoundly informed by the tragic consequences of Hitler's inferno, *A Breed Apart* offers poignant accounts of Professor Hoffman's long sojourn in Europe's DP camps, her hope-filled passage to the United States, and her resolute effort to transcend exilic limitations. **Furthermore, her personal experiences provide yet another unique example of the resiliency of the Jewish people** by showing how she established a family, continuously perfected her skills as a Yiddish writer, and passed on the rich heritage of Yiddish and Yiddishkayt to her students at Columbia University."

—Asher Z. Milbauer, Professor English/Director of Exile Studies Program, FIU

"Every Jew has a story but not every Jew is an accomplished writer and storyteller. Miriam Hoffman's memoir takes us on **a journey of the heartbreaks and triumphs** that Jews have experienced during the last eight decades, the Holocaust, the Soviet Gulag, the establishment of the state of Israel, and her survival and thriving in the United States. **She and her son Avi have been a major advocates for the Yiddish language and Yiddish culture. A wonderful read.**"

—Arnold Richards, Former Chairman of the Board, YIVO Institute for Jewish Research

"The agony of the Holocaust did not end in 1945; the DP camps existed for another five years. With a keen eye and great intelligence, Miriam Hoffman takes us into one of those camps. She shows the spirit of Jews, deeply—very deeply—injured and distressed human beings rebuilding their lives, their religion, and their *Yiddishkayt*. *A Breed Apart* **is truly an inspiring book. A must read!**"

—Rabbi Bruce Warshal, Past Chair, State of Florida Holocaust Task Force

"Miriam Hoffman's book *A Breed Apart* **is a remarkable and very engaging memoir** that chronicles the author's rise from a youth in the slave labor camps and the gulags of the Soviet Union under Stalin, through a five-year sojourn in a displaced persons camp in Germany after the war, to her immigration to the Bronx. Miriam's personal odyssey parallels and encapsulates the fate of the Yiddish language, and Yiddish culture, or *Yiddishkayt,* in the twentieth century. Ms. Hoffman has contributed and continues to contribute to the ongoing life of Yiddish culture and language in America, where she has for many years taught Yiddish at Columbia University. **For the Jews, throughout history, success often has meant to have just barely survived in a hostile world. Ms. Hoffman's success in life is much more than that, and her book is a testimonial to her life and career as an exemplar of the grit and resilience of *A Breed Apart*.**"

—Dr. Robert Paul, Charles Howard Candler Professor, Emory University

A
Breed Apart
Reflections of a Young Refugee

A Miraculous Escape from Russia: From DP Camp to Columbia University and Beyond

---

PROFESSOR MIRIAM HOFFMAN

YIDDISHKAYT PRESS
CORAL SPRINGS, FLORIDA

Published by

Yiddishkayt Press

A Division of The Yiddishkayt Initiative, Inc.

Coral Springs, Florida
www.YiddishkaytInitiative.org
www.MiriamHoffman.com

*The photos used in this book are reprinted courtesy of
the Mendl & Miriam Hoffman Archive*

ISBN: 978-0-9993365-0-2 (B&W)
978-0-6929269-4-9 (Color)

Editor: Carol Killman Rosenberg • www.carolkillmanrosenberg.com
Cover and interior: Gary A. Rosenberg • www.garyarosenberg.com

Printed in the United States of America

The founding statute of the International Refugee Organization (IRO) defines a Displaced Person (DP) as one who, as a result of acts of brutality, racism, bigotry, and atrocities, has been uprooted from his/her homeland or permanent dwelling place, or one who was forced into slave labor, or one who as a result of religious or political discrimination was driven from their permanent dwelling place.

To my father, Chaim Schmulewitz, writer, satirist, and humorist, whose feuilletonistic and satiric style of writing graced the Yiddish press *Undzer Weg* (Our Way) in Munich, Germany, between 1946 and 1949. His were mostly episodes of our Displaced Persons (DP) Camp Life from the perspective of an adult. I have translated from the Yiddish some of his articles that deal with our life inside of the DP camp and have incorporated them into this work. Chapters reflecting my father's contributions include his byline.

Contents

⟋

Foreword

Miriam Hoffman is a rare bird. Few Jewish children as young as she was during World War II survived the Holocaust, and fewer still grew to become writers in their adult lives. And among those few who did, how many have been so articulately bilingual, having mastered both Yiddish and English in a style that is at once idiomatic and ironic? How many found success as newspaper columnists, university language teachers and playwrights, all in one amazing life?

I've had the good fortune to have been a colleague of Hoffman in two of her three professional careers, and to occasionally observe her in the third from a close remove. All who've had that collegial relationship with her will surely attest to her energy and imagination, her unassuming, almost folksy manner, in her writing and stage direction as much as in her conversation with students and with peers. But make no mistake: her knowledge of her text runs deep.

Those qualities shine bright in the vignettes she recounts in this memoir. She can wonder at her mother's courage in writing daily encomiums to Stalin when her husband was in a Soviet prison and still recognize her inability to reach for a better life once she settled in America. She describes a child's death from hunger and its burial in a vermin-infested grave and still rejoices, a few years later, in the stylishness of a wedding dress she wouldn't deny herself. She shares the narrative with remembered stories published by her father in the Yiddish newspaper of the Displaced Persons' camp he wrote for, recalls his refusal, in a Soviet prison, to make a false confession even under torture, and recognizes his quiet devotion as he crosses borders to reunite with his wife and child after the war's end. But she also knows her own mind, even as a young girl, and knows when the time has come to leave her parents' home and make a life of her own.

Brief as it was, the four years she and her parents spent in a Jewish Displaced Persons' camp in Germany was surely the fulcrum and springboard of her life, as it is of this memoir. It was a time and place when all around her Jews were picking up the pieces of their shipwrecked lives. As individuals and as a community they did the miraculous work of *t'khias ha'maisim,* reviving the dead. Their families had been murdered, yet they took on the task of saving their families. In the relative safety of the refugee camps, and in the close company of other Jews who had suffered the same Gehinom, they spoke the languages of their childhood homes, married and gave birth, wrote and read newspapers, staged plays and concerts, prayed and learned, sent their children to school, organized demonstrations for a state for Jews, learned a craft, and treated themselves to the habits of a normal life. The miracle is that people who had witnessed what they had could do such things.

Miriam Hoffman was only nine when she and her parents arrived in the Hindenburg Kaserne DP camp in Ulm, Germany, and thirteen when they left it for America, but those four years were her finishing school. She went on to get a good formal education later in Yiddish and English in New York and in Miami, but her curiosity, her respect for her own culture, her own language, her own knowledge were forged early on, in those years. I invite you to trace what she did with those values by reading this remarkable memoir.

Samuel Norich, President of The Forward Association

The Young Author, Age 2

Author's Note

*W*hy are the Jewish people "A Breed Apart"? What is the nature of survival against all odds? I began my life as an infant under a severe regime in the Soviet Union, fleeing from Eastern to Western Europe mostly by foot, reaching the American Zone in post-war Germany, spending a childhood in a Displaced Persons Refugee Camp and finally touching American soil to become a successful educator, journalist and playwright.

Today, I still marvel at our past. How does a people pull itself together after such a catastrophe and go on living, go on creating and recreating itself, renewing itself and continuing to contribute to the world? Apparently, by rebuilding families, by raising children, erecting Yeshivas (religious academies), Jewish schools, libraries, Yiddish and Jewish Theaters, and publishing houses, and documenting the witness accounts of the Holocaust survivors.

Cultural Jewish life is not lost. What is lost are the six million slaughtered Jews, whose unborn future generations will forever deprive us of their contributions to Jewish life, culture and world civilization. Had those six million Jews been allowed to live and thrive, by now, there would have been 100 million Jews, among them our now lost scholars, professors, rabbis, doctors, artists, and so on.

It was Sam Levinson, the Jewish-American humorist, who once asked, "Who is a Jew?" And his answer was, "He who will have Jewish grandchildren." And I might as well add, I hope that our future generations will explore, seek out, and discover their Jewish roots and continue their own remarkable historical journey and legacy.

Yiddish Song from Author's Journal

PROLOGUE

My First Birth Certificate Out of Three

I was born in three installments, the first being in the Siberian town of Tobolsk, on June 26, 1936, where Father was incarcerated on trumped-up charges of espionage. There I was granted my first birth certificate.

When I was the tender age of one week, my father was released from prison and given permission to return to the same slave labor camp Slavuta in the Ural Mountains, where he had been previously arrested as a rabble-rouser. We arrived in the slave labor camp, where rumor had it that I was just born, and so I was granted my *second* birth certificate.

My third birth occurred in 1947, after the war, when I was eleven years old and stationed on the American zone in the DP camp (displaced persons refugee camp) named Hindenburg Kaserne in Ulm, Germany. That same year, the American embassy in Germany notified parents that their children would be denied entry to the United States since they were born under Soviet rule. It was the time of McCarthyism and the Communist scare. With the help of the "Joint Distribution Committee," it took no time for these children—including me—to be provided with a third birth certificate stating that we had been born in Poland *before* the Russian occupation.

Русская народная песня

	припев.
Слушайте друзья	Ривочка
Что я вам расскажу	моя красавица
Жил в Одессе	Я тебя люблю
Один еврей богатый	сильно горячо
Лучше он всех	И может
Еврейских дам	быть когда
Я любил брюнетку	Мы встретимся
Ривочку красотку	когда.
И был готов	И будешь
для ней всю	ты моя
жизнь отдать	Жена.
Он пел ей.	

Russian Song from Author's Journal

CHAPTER 1

On the Threshold
of My Pre-Birth (A Fantasy)

*B*efore discussing my coming of age in the displaced persons refugee camp, I would like to start out with my unexpected birth. It turns out that my parents met in one of the barracks for the young people in the Gulag's slave labor camp, where common life was co-ed. There they were put to work in the forests, cutting down trees to build more barracks for new, innocent Jewish youth from all over Europe with no prospects for a better life. It was the time of the Great Depression.

I was unaware of my whereabouts. "Where am I?" I inquired.

The angels chuckled. "Mirele, Pirele, silly goose! You're in seventh heaven, and about to break loose."

"About to break loose?" I quipped with a smirk. "You mean I haven't been hatched yet?"

"No!" They cackled into their sprawling wings. "Chicks are hatched, babies are born. Look down and you'll see your mother trudging around, her belly up to her nose."

"Which one is my mother?" I wanted to know.

They pointed out a she-person waddling like a duck from side to side.

"I refuse to be born!" I protested. "I was on the spot! No one asked me if I agree."

1

Tola Neuhaus (Author's mother)

The angels squinted their milk-soppy eyes, echoing Andromeda's spell, restfully snoozing along the misty nebula.

With a stubborn nod of my head, I stood firm. "I'll mount the Golden Peacock and ride into the Galactic-Circle. Let my mother give birth to some other chump, but not me."

"Idle threats," puffed the angel Sheyndele, the Heavenly Chatterbox, "no one is asking you. No one cares what you think . . ."

"Oh, yeah?" I stuck my tongue out at her. "Then before it happens, I want to have a chat with the earth-woman who I will be calling 'Mother' for the rest of my life. Let's see if this whole birth thing is worth the trouble."

The angels reconvened. Amid all the fluttering of yeas and nays, it was decided to grant me my wish. They pointed out my earth-mother, set me down in the middle of her dream, and I dissolved into the Milky Way. I planted a kiss on the tip of my mother's nose. She groaned, "Oy! I feel the baby, is it time?"

"No, Mama," I assured her. "It's not time yet. I'm not ready."

"Woe is me," she moaned in her sleep. "What do you mean you're not ready? I've been dragging you around for an entire nine months. I can't take it anymore!

"Mama, I don't want to be born. Every day I do somersaults over the billowy clouds. In the evening, I string glittering little stars into a necklace. Up here we have a waterfall, and we can slide all the way from the very top of the nebulous clouds to the soft, mossy, elliptical galaxy below. And when the angel *Nekhome* rinses out her lingerie, we get to blow soap bubbles all day long. The butterflies get into the act, but every time one lands on a bubble, it bursts, and then I cry. But *Nekhome* distracts me with crescent lollypops dipped in honeydew, and with stories of fireflies in June, with cows jumping over the moon. So you see why I don't want to be born. Besides, I'll lose my heavenly circle of friends and never stop longing for them."

"Don't make trouble, little one," Mama demanded.

"I won't make trouble, Mama, I promise! But before I step into the spotlight, I want to see if this whole exertion is worth it."

"What do you mean 'worth it'? Who says you have a choice?"

"I do," I said while poking her on the left side of her belly. "I'm privileged, so I demand to know where you intend to give birth to me!"

"What do you mean 'where'? Right here, my child, in Siberia, where your father languishes in a dingy prison cell and your mother is faint with hunger."

"Mama!" I pressed on, "Why, of all places, Siberia? Why not America?"

"Child!" she cried. "They're talking war out there, and you feed me funny lines?"

"War? What is war, Mama?"

"War, my child, is when humans slaughter each other like cattle."

"And you want me to be born at this given moment in time? I'd better postpone my opening number until the proverbial lion will lie down with the lamb."

"There will never be an end to war, little one. Mankind has a short memory."

"How many wars will it take before the human race kills itself off, Mama?"

"God only knows, so why don't you make a quantum leap and crack that soap bubble?"

Speechless for a moment, my mother lay still on her narrow plank in the freezing hovel. Suddenly she got up, straightened out her clothes, threw on a heavy shawl, and stepped outside. The sun was glittering in the melting snow.

The sparkly ice was melting. The frozen Irtysh River had begun to crack, and boats could be seen in the distance. My mother marched with defiant steps straight to the local Commissariat headquarters of the NKVD. She opened the door with a flair and determination, stationing herself in front of the top uniform.

"Hear me out and hear me good, Comrade Karitch," she announced loud and clear. "By the looks of me, you can tell I'm about to go into labor."

"You're not the first and not the last," he said while blowing *makhorka* tobacco from his pipe. "Every day some female gives birth here in the Siberian *Tyga*, this wilderness."

"Yes," my mother uttered, "but this child came to me in a dream and said that she doesn't want to be born here in the frozen tundra! She said this is not a place for babies."

"Neither is it for adults," Karitch snickered in mockery. "The baby came to you in a dream you say?"

"Not just that," Mother went on. "The baby gave me a full description of seventh heaven, down to the detailed account of how they frolic there with butterflies and soap bubbles, how they slide down silvery waterfalls and listen as *Sheyndele* the Chatterbox spins her golden tales."

Karitch and the other officials quickly realized that this lady was not all there, that she was overwrought as she was overdue, and that they would wind up with a madwoman and a child on their hands. They hastily prepared an executive order to waive all espionage charges against her husband and granted her a petition that confirmed that, as soon as the baby made an appearance, she could pack up her measly belongings and clear out, along with her husband and newborn child. From there, they could return to the slave labor camp where they had been picked up and transported to Siberia on trumped-up charges.

Mother was in seventh heaven, and that's where I made her acquaintance.

"Mama!" I pulled at her apron strings. "I need to know one more thing before I consent to be born. Don't forget that up here, time is eternal, so I want to know how long my life span is going to be in that grizzly world. And don't forget, up here I was blessed with a "sensillum" receptor . . ."

And before I knew it, I was plunged into a cavernous canal. Not known for being a good swimmer, I tossed about in the rolling current, drowning and choking.

"Where on earth am I?" I wondered, barely out of seventh heaven and already dazed and confused. The storm waves subsided enough for me to catch my breath, but within minutes, I was sucked into a whirlpool, swallowed up by the slimy swamp.

Down I went, faster and faster. And then, out of nowhere, I heard my mother's voice: "Let me out of here! I have had enough!"

How interesting, I mused. *She was just imploring me to appear, and already she regrets the entire thing.* Suddenly I slid out and . . . I remember nothing more.

CHAPTER 2

Chaim, My Father

*M*y father, Chaim Schmulewitz, was born in Lodz, Poland, in 1906. At the age of three, he lost his twenty-three-year-old mother, Mirla, after whom I am named, and remained motherless with his little sister, Rokhelle, who was at that time one and a half. Their grandparents refused to deal with the two children, causing their father, Avrum Berish, to remarry. Their new stepmother, who specialized in wig-making, came into the family with a son of her own. At the outbreak of World War I in 1914, my grandfather, Avrum, was drafted into the Polish army, never to return.

Father attended Hebrew school but grew up in the streets. Once he reached the ripe old age of ten, he got himself a job as an errand boy for Lazar Kahn's newspaper *Der Lodzer Folksblat* (*The Lodz Folk-Paper*), a Yiddish daily. He eventually became a typesetter and printer, working steadily until the 1930s, when the world was engulfed in the Great Depression.

Chaim Schmulewitz (Author's father)

CHAPTER 3

Gelleh, My Father's First and Only Love Interest

Father was, at one time, a handsome and elegant young man, tall, with broad shoulders and a forelock of curly red hair. He loved flirting with the girls. Many young women set their sights on him, but he cared only for one—Gelleh. She boasted a pair of hot, flaming eyes and a head of blond silken hair. She was sensuous, agile, and clever. Her mother kept close watch over her and commented on every move she made—"Don't go out with this one, don't hang out with that one"—but she made no objections to my father's courting of her daughter.

Father worked in the editor's office and had made a good living until the difficult thirties crept up on Poland. In those days, the Jewish youth felt as though it had been trapped in a cage. Where could they flee when the countries all over the world closed their doors to them, including both Americas?

The Soviet Union enticed them with promises of a good life: "Come, children!" they preached. "Come, precious ones! Help build a new world, a free world, where the worker is the boss! Whoever wants to put shoulder to the wheel can be assured a golden future."

What was one to do?

In the midst of it all, my father's beloved Gelleh broke the sad news to her lover that she and her family had booked passage on a boat heading for Canada. Canada was always in need of skillful tailors, carpenters, and mechanics.

Gelleh promised that as soon as she arrived, she would send for him, and they would get married and live out their lives in total bliss. They swore eternal love to each other; they wept and they moaned. My father gave her a golden watch as a sign of their love and accompanied her to the railroad station. Their love letters flew back and forth as if on the wings of eagles.

A year passed, and Gelleh's letters took on a different tone. She had become acquainted with a young man, and they were "keeping company." She wrote that her mother "feels that it is for the best." Of course, this was my father's private tragedy. In the meantime, Father's newspaper shut down. That's when my father fell prey to the Soviet propaganda posters and leaflets spreading their distorted truth all over his birthplace in Lodz. The Soviet leaflets were enticing the young ones with promises of a free education, work galore, and above all human rights and a brave new world.

He informed his sister, stepmother, and stepbrother that he had made up his mind to seek his fortune in the Soviet Union. He took off, smuggled illegally across the Polish-Russian border.

This was the time when Jewish girls realized that their chances for marriage were very slim—they had no dowry and not many prospects—so many of them took off illegally to the Soviet Union to get a husband.

At the time of the Great Depression, thousands of Jewish youth of Poland, Ukraine, Lithuania, Romania, Hungary, and even North and South America paid smugglers to take them across the border to the Soviet Union, where the cattle cars were ready in waiting to escort them straight to the slave labor camps. This was the Soviet Union's answer to free labor: they betrayed the innocent youth, who found themselves behind barbed wire and bayonets.

Rukhl Schmulewitz Poznanski (Author's aunt)

Rukhl Schmulewitz Poznanski (Bottom Row, 2nd from left)

CHAPTER 4

Tola, My Mother

My mother, Tola-Bronya (Tiltche Brayndl) Neuhaus, on the other hand, was one of four siblings. Her father, Yehuda Zaynvl, was a glazier and a weaver. He agreed with Karl Marx that "religion is the opium of the masses," so he banned anything that dealt with religion and tradition in the house.

Tola Schmulewitz Neuhaus (Author's mother)

Yehuda Zanvil Neuhaus
(Author's grandfather)

Rukhl (Grandmother) and
Golde (Aunt) Neuhaus

My maternal grandmother, Rukhl, was a tubercular woman, submissive and subservient to her husband. When word reached her that her husband, my grandfather, was having an affair with another woman, she asked three of her children to snoop around and follow him. They returned with the bitter news that the rumor was true, so Rukhl urged the children to escape their father's wrath and make their way to the Soviet Union, where life after the Revolution, she reasoned, must be beautiful, free, and vibrant, and in search of young and skillful workers.

That is how my mother's older sister, Nakhe, and eighteen-year-old brother, Avrum, wound up the first ones in the family to become victims of the Gulag, the penal system of the USSR, which consisted of a network of labor camps. From time to time, they were handed postcards to write home, describing how wonderful life was in the Soviet Union. It enticed my mother to follow their venture, and two years later, she was off to the Land of Oz.

CHAPTER 5

The Slave Labor Camp Slavuta in the Caucasus Under Soviet Rule

The slave labor camp housed the young people in barracks that they built themselves by the sweat of their brows. The barracks were co-ed, and free love was the only thing that was free in the Soviet Union, especially for the men and women who shared the same barracks.

There were no marriages performed in the slave labor camps, let alone Jewish ones. The young girls usually lost their menstrual periods due to the lack of nutrition and vitamins, which didn't apply to my mother as she discovered she was pregnant with me and became overwhelmed with fear.

Once Mother found herself under barbed wire and was handed the postcards to write home, she decided to write that, "Life is beautiful for all, though I haven't seen Berl the baker for several days now, and Yosl the butcher shows up quite seldom. Otherwise, we live in paradise." This was an indication that there was little bread or meat to be found in the camp.

To Mother's parents in Lodz, several years before World War II, it was a great blow; they knew full well they were responsible for their children's demise. Once the war broke out, they refrained from sending their youngest daughter, Golde, to this place of misery. Little

13

did they know what was awaiting them; instead of escaping to the Soviet Union, they all met their deaths in Auschwitz-Birkenau.

After several years of this misery, my father, a most naive young man in his twenties, decided to question this slave labor camp arrangement. "What are we doing here?" he wanted to know. "We came here to work, to build, to learn the language, the culture, to be free, enjoy human rights, but instead . . ."

This caused a great commotion and uproar in the barrack that he shared with dozens of other innocent victims.

For his outburst, Father was immediately sent off to prison, to the Siberian town of Tobolsk. My mother followed him, realizing that she was about to encounter immense difficulties in her life on her way to this frozen tundra.

As her pregnancy progressed, she was a frequent patron at the headquarters of the NKVD, the Soviet version of the CIA, crying, pleading, begging them to free her innocent husband and let them return at least to the slave labor camp where the weather was much milder and the birth would be easier. My mother was small in stature, in her twenties, a girl with thick, curly black hair and coal-dark eyes, extremely determined to convince the high officials of her despair.

Day after day, she was at the headquarters, pleading with the officials to have pity, if not upon her, at least on the unborn infant that would surely not survive this frozen Siberian wilderness.

CHAPTER 6

Broken Chains

After a while, the Soviet officials in the city of Tobolsk relented. They could no longer stand my mother's nagging and pleading, so they assured her that at the end of June, when the Irtysh River thawed and the first boats arrived, they would release her husband, allowing them to leave with the infant baby and head back to the slave labor camp—the very origin of Father's harsh punishment for his innocent inquiry.

The military officials of Tobolsk kept their promise. As soon as I was born, my father was released. I was provided with my first birth certificate, as I mentioned earlier. At the infirmary in Tobolsk, the nurse told Father that I was a boy. Of course, Father was elated with the good news. The following morning he was rightly informed I was a girl. He grimaced and cried out, "Oh, no! Nooooo!"

Finally, the anticipated boat arrived at the end of June, and the three of us (I was between one and two weeks old at the time) boarded that boat returning back to Slavuta in the Caucasus, where the nurses, convinced that I had just been born, extended my mother a new diaper, a little blanket, and my second birth certificate.

CHAPTER 7

Lost in the Quagmire
of the Soviet Union

Once my parents were released from the slave labor camp, a year later, they began their journey through the little villages and towns of the Soviet Union, where my father was constantly in danger of a renewed arrest due to the Soviet policy and style of life: everyone was suspected of espionage—the entire Soviet Union, under Stalin's stark-raving, psychopathic insanity.

Finally, after searching for weeks, Father found work in a small town newspaper, where he observed one worker pointing to the portrait of Stalin on the wall and quipping, "Hang the bastard closer to the fireplace. Maybe he'll warm up!" The next morning, the worker was arrested and gone.

My father decided to skip town once again and look up the residences of my mother's brother and sister, who lived in the big city of Saratov in Central Russia. By the time my mother and I, still only about a year old, arrived in Saratov, both of my uncles had already been inmates for several years in slave labor camps in Siberia. Nevertheless, we stayed in Saratov until our escape.

When my father was finally released for the umpteenth time from the prison in Saratov, he was invited by the NKVD (KGB) to meet in a neighboring park. There an agent instructed him, "Now that you are free, your task is to inform on the Jews who secretly frequent a hidden synagogue. All we want from you is to know who they are and their names. If you don't comply, you'll go back to prison."

My father knew full well that all synagogues had been shut down, so his answer was determent and swift. "I am not a religious man, I don't pray and don't frequent synagogues."

"Then you show up in their secret prayer houses or basements and pretend you are religious."

"You can arrest me again and again," my father replied, "but I don't know any religious Jews."

Arrested again and again, his conscience was clear. Others did comply under strain, not only because of weakness of character, but because their lives were at stake. Once imprisoned, Father was handed a document, a prewritten confession to sign. He refused and suffered the consequences. He was beaten and confined to a cell, fed salty herring, and deprived of water.

Chaim Schmulewitz in Russia

17

CHAPTER 8

Destruction
of the Jewish Culture

*B*y the late twenties and throughout the thirties, forties, and fifties, Jewish culture in the Soviet Union was already on the brink of decline. First went the places of worship, followed by ceremonial weddings, circumcisions, celebration of holidays, and the baking of matzoh. All were strictly forbidden. Anyone caught breaking these decrees was sentenced to slave labor for ten years.

The network of Yiddish schools, as well as the Jewish cultural and art worlds were at an end. The Yiddish press, with its dozens of publications of sacred and secular books, newspapers, magazines, and scholarly works, were all destroyed, as well as their Jewish language, Yiddish. At the same time, the Moscow State Yiddish Theater as well as the dozens of traveling Yiddish theater troupes throughout the Soviet Union also dissolved.

Shloyme (Solomon) Mikhoels (1890–1948), the legendary founder, artistic director, and actor of the Moscow State Yiddish Theater, was the envy of every artist in the Soviet Union. Shakespearean actors from the "Old Vic" in London used to come and marvel at Mikhoels' "King Lear" in Yiddish. Stalin envied the world-famous Mikhoels, and as an act of revenge, he ordered his execution in 1948. A truck followed Mikhoels to Minsk when he was on his way to a performance and crushed him to death in the street.

Yiddish actors, poets, writers, artists were in jeopardy from the 1930s to the 1950s when every one of them was either incarcerated in the Lubyanka prison in Moscow, shot, or sent to Siberia. The Jewish world capitulated.

Yiddish Bundist School, Lodz Poland, 1946
(Author is Bottom Row, 1st from left)

CHAPTER 9

Physical and Mental Torture

The last time Father was arrested, he was interrogated and tortured, and his captors tried to force him to sign a confession stating that he had come to the city of Saratov to poison the wells and commit treason by bombing the covered market in town. He refused to sign. Most of the innocent victims signed, because they could not withstand the interrogations and torture. But not my father; even though he was beaten and tortured, he refused to sign.

Ironically, weeks later, the prison Director was accused of espionage and all those who had signed confessions were taken away, while Father and the others who refused to sign a confession were released.

Mother, Father, and I lived in the dingy, freezing basement of a hovel. Staring at us was the one little window, covered with frost and ice. I was constantly bedridden, too cold to get out of bed. Our wall was full of cracks and holes. When my mother was away and my father would return from a day's work, all he had to do was poke a stick through the crack in the wall and wake me up to open the door. I was only four years old. We lived in this dump with another family, a mother with her two teenaged sons. It seems their father absconded and escaped to Mexico never to return.

Out of frustration, my mother decided to sit down and write a letter to Comrade Stalin, His "Eminence," the Greatest Commander and Chief, the Prodigious Father of the Nation and Savior of his people, describing the conditions under which we lived. She wrote daily, while everyone around us became convinced my mother had lost her mind. It was almost an entire page of accolades to this inhumane monster.

Author and Parents in Russia

CHAPTER 10

My Mother's Quirky Brainstorm

*W*hat, you may ask, was the nature of the relationship between my mother and Stalin? The answer is that both of them made use of the same railway tracks—he on his way to the Kremlin, and she on her way to the Gulag. This intimate kinship was not to be lightly dismissed, because in fact, this grizzly old man with the thick and alarming mustache was attempting to convince half the people of the world that he was "The Benevolent Father of a Nation," and following his own line of reasoning, didn't that inadvertently make my mother his daughter?

But what did he have against her? Nothing! So why the Gulag? Though busily engaged in the distribution of hell on earth, Stalin didn't fail to provide for my mother. He had guaranteed her a fair share of jails and labor camps, starvation, and misery. This combination of catastrophes might have continued indefinitely were it not for my mother's determination. She declared unequivocally that such tactics would not work with her. On the contrary, she would teach "The Father of the Nation" that you don't fool around with *Tola Bronya Neuhaus, Schmulewitz Yihide Zavlevnovna.* (In Russia, one must always supply the maiden name, the married name, and the father's name on every document for identification.)

CHAPTER 11

Mother's Letter to the "Grand Old Executioner," Comrade Stalin

*W*hen push came to shove, my mother didn't hesitate; she rolled up her sleeves, took pen in hand, and showed Stalin what she was made of.

It seems that my mother was a hotshot with the pen, and she deluged His Excellency Comrade Stalin with her correspondence. Her approach was unique, while all her letters often began with an elaborate salutation:

> *Most Exalted Father of the Nation, who has assured humanity of fairness and justice and freedom, who has sacrificed himself for the working class, put them on their feet and made of them what they are today. Believe me, they will remember it as long as they live. Loyal protector of the persecuted and pursuer, guardian of the masses, our faithful redeemer from the yoke of capitalism—how can I recount your greatness and accomplishments?*
>
> *There is none whom to compare you within the annals of the human race. One can only be left speechless by your achievements. Who is there to sing your praises? You are one of a kind, unique in the Universe.*

But though you have provided for everyone, you have forgotten me . . . me and my innocent husband, who is rotting in the jails constantly for absolutely no reason whatsoever. You have forgotten also about my tiny little girl, who lies ailing in a dark cellar and doesn't see the light of day. Why do I deserve all this, dear Father of the Nations? You must arrange for my husband's speedy release and provide us with a decent home of our own. I know full well how busy you are; your plate is full, what with Smolensk and Stalingrad. Nevertheless, I don't see how you can be indifferent to my plight! I realize also that you consider some matters to be greater priorities, but I won't stop writing until you pay attention to my quandary. As soon as I finish this letter, I'm going to sit myself down and write a second and a third letter; I won't rest until you respond.

Send my warmest regards to everyone in the Kremlin.

Your loyal citizen,
Tola Bronya Neuhaus, Schmulewitz Yihide Zavlevnovna

Have you ever heard of such boldness? My mother's neighbors warned her that Stalin would make her eat dust, but that didn't deter her. She continued to write her daily sermon to Stalin and kept an eye out for the postman. Who knows? Maybe she would hear from the old scoundrel after all.

Time passed with no response forthcoming. But my mother didn't give up that easily. As dependable as the sun rose each morning, she dispatched her daily letters to the Father of the Nation. Most of the pages were covered with descriptions of his awesome majesty. And, at the very bottom, she would add a couple of little lines:

It's a matter of life and death. We will soon expire from the damp and frozen basement, which is our abode. Please provide us with a decent home.

One bright morning, a letter arrived from the highest Soviet authority, namely, the Kremlin, which read:

Dear Madam Tola Bronya Neuhaus, Schmulewitz
Yihide Zavlevnovna,

"We have taken your daily letters into consideration
and have decided to investigate this entire matter. In the
meantime, we will re-examine the charges against your
blameless husband and provide you with a home. Show this
letter to the Chief of Police in your district and you will get
the key to your new habitat, located on Astrakhanskaya
Ulitsa (street), number 27, in the city of Saratov.
And remember that you are living in the land of freedom
and justice, where Iosif Vissarionovich Stalin himself provides
for every citizen personally. We are doing this by his kind
benevolence with this one provision: stop writing letters because
the Father of the Nation has a weak nervous system.

I cannot describe in my own words the great happiness that must certainly have pervaded our freezing cold basement that day, for I was too young to preserve all the memories of that occasion. When my mother, however, was reminded of this particular day, she would swell with pride.

A short time later, Father was released once again. As soon as my father was out of prison, we caught the tram, rode to the district headquarters, and, with a police escort, went off to get the first look at our new one-room abode.

CHAPTER 12

Our New Domicile

How can I express it? The house actually had a presentable façade; it was made of brick walls and a roof. When we got to our designated door, however, a seal was posted on it, issued by the district supreme court, which informed every person in the building that this room was confiscated for three months time and that anyone entering through this door and breaking the seal would be arrested.

What a shock! All our joy fizzled out. But my mother didn't get discouraged. Luckily, the house had all its rooms on the ground floor, so she began with a scare tactic. After all she was in the possession of a document from the highest Soviet authorities. Stalin himself gave the authorization for her to get this place at once as if to say, "Remember, you don't play games with Stalin."

So the court took another look at the red-stamped official letter from the Kremlin, blinked their eyes, and shrugged their shoulders, utterly unable to figure out the connection between this diminutive, attractive young woman and the great Father of the Nation.

The commandant in charge of order in our city observed carefully the "confiscated" notice with the seal on the door, scratched his bald spot, and could not come up with a favorable solution.

"And what about Stalin?" My mother shoved the letter into his face. "Bear in mind," she said, "that I frequently exchange letters with the Father of the Nation, and I will be forced to write to him that his word counts for naught here."

Upon hearing this refrain, the commandant turned white as chalk and trembled from head to toe. In the meantime, my mother went out into the inner yard and located our window on the ground floor where a tall tree was growing. She clambered up the tree, forced the window open, and crawled inside our designated room. The commandant reluctantly stayed behind.

Mother looked out the window and cried out triumphantly, "There you have it! Two sunny windows! A gem of a room. Stalin is quite an expert when it comes to beautiful homes."

The room even had a built-in French stove made out of bricks, with a chimney!

"It will be a small inconvenience because of the sealed door, but that's really no big deal. We will be able to crawl through the window, my child would be able to go to school through the window, we will go to work through the window. Aside from this drawback, we can live here in great comfort compared to the frozen basement!"

If Stalin orders, the deed shall be done.

My mother was in seventh heaven. Such a stroke of luck! She had finagled her way to acquiring four walls and a roof, an airy domicile with two windows, full of sunlight. Little by little, we became accustomed to crawling up and down the tree trunk. Was that supposed to be a disadvantage to a little girl? Hardly! I don't remember how long the climbing and crawling went on, but I do recall one thing: the day that we opened the sealed door was a day of mourning for me.

As soon as we settled into our new home, Father and Mother began dreaming of making a final exit from the land that had been so ingeniously and malevolently founded on "freedom, equality, and justice for all." Most important, they wanted to be rid of the sharp claws belonging to the "Father of the Nation."

We settled in, happily knowing full well that we were the most fortunate family to live in a house that had two sunny windows.

CHAPTER 13

The Russian City of Saratov

*B*etween the ages of three and eight, I lived in the Russian city of Saratov, centrally located along the River Volga with a population of a million inhabitants, where life for us children was shaky and unstable due to the raging war.

At the start of World War II, which broke out when I was only three, all the parents started out by digging a pit in our inner courtyard for safety, but when the bombings began, no one dared to hide in the open pit. Instead, we sat out the bombings in the house, covering the window with the only mattress we had in case of shrapnel.

Our city of Saratov housed a goodly number of gas refineries, and thus it became one of the epicenters of the German bombings. The sight of our city burning all around is an indelible memory in my mind. The cries of women who had lost their husbands and loved ones rang in our house throughout the war.

But we children just kept on playing, paying little mind to what was happening, as if to say, "It doesn't concern us." Deep in our hearts, we knew there was a war on and people were being killed, but we had no idea what constituted death as long as we felt safe.

During the war, all my friends were between the ages of three and five. They were Russians of different ethnicities. I was Jewish, but at the time I didn't really know what that meant, since all religions were banned in the Soviet Union. At the age of five, I had no clue why I was a Jew or what a Jew was. My parents spoke Yiddish in the house, and I answered back in Russian, embarrassed to speak Yiddish in front of my Russian friends.

I spent my childhood in that house until we made our miraculous escape from the "Russian Paradise" just one month after the end of World War II, leaving behind that sunny room with the two windows and the tall tree that I loved to crawl up and slide down so much. This childhood vision is imbedded in my mind like the picture of our "outhouse."

Urination was done into a bucket during the night, and in the morning it was spilled into the wooden outhouse. Our house was inhabited by at least thirty dwellers, three generations to a room. Every one of them needed to eliminate in the outhouse, which stood close to the garbage dump that was never cleaned. All winter long, the excrement was frozen. Once the warm spring arrived, the elder men (the younger men were at the front) would come out with spades and dig a canal underneath our outhouse into our front yard that stopped at the gate to the house. By this time, the bulk of the excrement was melted and spilled into the provisional canal. The men would immediately cover it up with the dug-up ground and let it rest.

At the end of spring, flowers and berries began to grow above the canal of excrement, and for us children, it was a season of great joy, eating the berries of many colors. This was one of the pleasures we associated with spring.

CHAPTER 14

Death: A New Discovery

When I was five, I saw the corpse of a soldier in front of our house. He lay there for days until the smell was unbearable. I suddenly understood the difference between life and death.

War, especially death, comes as a rude awakening at any age. I remember a physical reaction when our city was bombed. My entire body experienced a convulsion, similar to an earthquake, knowing that at any given moment it could erupt and toss us into eternity. Once we came to that conclusion, life took on a greater meaning.

I remember Mother waking me up one morning from my deep sleep, which made me angry; after all, it was Sunday. She lit a match and threw it onto the wooden chips in the stove. In a minute, the oven began to crackle as the fire intensified.

I heard a tap at the door. It was my best friend Yurka, who lived across the hall. He asked me to come outside.

What could it be? I wondered.

The glass of milk my mother placed in front of me was too hot. I waited until it cooled off and the thin top skin of cream appeared. I stuck my finger into the glass, wound the milk-skin around my finger, and popped it into my mouth, skin, finger, and all. All at once, I slid out through the open window and down the tree trunk I went. Is there a better way to leave the house, I ask you?

Ours was a spacious inner courtyard. Yurka was chasing a chicken. All the chickens from the neighborhood used to fly over our wooden fence and pick on whatever they could put their beaks into. Sometimes the chickens had to fight off the starving dogs and cats that came in search of food in our garbage dump.

I remember Yurka suddenly stopped chasing the petrified chicken, wiped his nose on his shirtsleeve, and started running toward me.

"You know," he said, "yesterday my little brother Genka died, and today is his funeral. Mother and some of the neighbors put him into a little wooden casket, nailed it down, and now we are waiting for the truck to take us to the cemetery."

It struck me as the beginning of a new game. I said, "Yurka! Can I come along?"

"Of course! You're my best friend, aren't you?"

I nodded. "And what about Ninka?" I asked. "She's also our best friend."

"Sure, go ahead and call her, too."

I left Yurka behind and ran breathlessly through the other entrance to our house. Ninka's door was always wide open. Her mother had just finished washing her hair. She poured a quart of kerosene on Ninka's head to eradicate the lice, drying her hair with a towel. Ninka's mother, a wide and heavy-set woman with a horse-like face, always looked like she slept on a sack of beans. She kept on cursing and mumbling to herself, "They'll be the end of me yet, the kids and their lice."

Holding my nose to block the smell of the kerosene, I called out, "Ninka! Coming out? You want to see a graveyard? Genka's funeral is today. He is nailed in a box and the truck is coming for him soon."

Her eyes twinkled with excitement. Ninka showed me a small brush and began rubbing her lips; she wanted her lips to look red. Then she took a piece of cotton and rubbed it in the whitewash on the wall. "This is how my big sister does it when she wants to be beautiful, so give me your cheeks." She laughed. "We'll be the prettiest little girls at the funeral."

By now, our courtyard was buzzing with people, both Yurka's

family and our neighbors. Yurka's mother's face was awash with tears. His grandmother, a small and frail woman in a long and colorful skirt, spread wide in case she needed to pee while carrying on a conversation, was wobbly on her feet.

The old shoemaker, who lived with his young wife and infant girl, standing next to us was grumpy as usual. His face resembled a puffed-up balloon. He was almost deaf, so everyone had to shout into his ear. He was the one who used to shake the tree in our yard while I was on top of it, eating the yellow little flowers off its branches. He used to yell, "The Jews will eat us out of the country!"

Of course, I didn't know who he was referring to, and if he meant me, I didn't know that "we Jews" had such huge appetites. When the truck arrived, the old shoemaker lifted up Genka's little casket and held it between his dirty fingers. Passing our window and heading toward the fence, the procession followed him into the waiting truck. He put the coffin down with great care as if he were finishing a new pair of shoes. One by one, everybody filed into the massive truck.

Yurka's mother started shouting, "Get a move on! The truck driver is impatient." Then she brushed past everybody in silence. Ninka grabbed my arm and off we went to the cemetery.

The truck made screeching sounds as it drove. We passed a little brook, hiding among the bushes that ran along the narrow path where the Gypsies had settled for the summer. We passed several Gypsy girls nursing newborn babies on the sidewalk. Barefoot Gypsy children played in dirty puddles. An old Gypsy woman ran after our truck, shouting, "Your fortune told, very cheap!"

We passed the circus with its red-domed roof, where inside, ducks danced and roosters dueled one another with toy guns that shot cotton bullets. Just the previous week, Father had taken me to the circus, where dogs and cats dashed around hauling tiny stagecoaches in which rabbits were riding.

We approached the railway tracks. The military base where my father worked as manager of a military supply depot stood nearby. Everybody in that factory wore a military uniform. I tugged on Yurka's sleeve.

"Remember when your father came home one day all dressed up in his soldier's uniform?" I asked. "He had a real gun on him. I also remember how your father loved to shoot birds singing in the trees, and we used to catch the dead little critters, dig a pit, and give them a fine burial."

Ninka interrupted, "Remember the time when the fathers were all home before the war, they would gather outside every evening, put on their heavy boots, take their heap of greasy fishing rods and nets and go down to the Volga River to fish? We danced around the campfire in the courtyard waiting for them to return, soaking wet with the foul smell of fish."

"They would empty their nets and throw the lobsters and the fish on the ground, and the mothers would start scraping their slippery shells, throwing them into the big kettle to cook over the outdoor fire. And everybody would eat and the fathers would drink bottles of vodka till they got drunk, then they would sleep it off on the grass till morning."

"Hey, look!" Yurka interrupted. "The Vshiviy Bazaar!"

The Vshiviy Bazaar, or Flea Market, carried merchandise displayed both on wagon-carts and burlap sacks on the ground. There were Samovars, wooden spoons, full barrels of herring and sour cabbage, bearded goats, and Moscow chocolate. We children felt joyful at the sight of all the fascinating items that seemed to be calling out to us.

All at once, we approached a wide-open gate. There was no fence around the cemetery. On both sides of the gates, beggars accosted our truck, toothless old women that looked like frightening witches. Squinting eyes gazed at us over monstrous, gaping, toothless mouths. They approached us with prayers. "In the name of the Lord, make Christ happy! Bring joy to our Lord! Give something, anything..."

Now I was sorry that I had come along. I held on tightly to Yurka's hand, thinking, *What if Mother will look for me? After all, I never told her where I was going.*

The truck stopped. The driver said he'd wait for us while we all jumped off the truck. The deaf shoemaker grabbed the little casket with his puffy hands, put it on his shoulder, and started out. We all followed him slowly through the graveyard in cold silence.

"Look!" Yurka squeezed my hand. "Dead soldiers carried on stretchers to be buried."

"My poor Fyedushka!" Yurka's mother cried, referring to her fallen husband, and then let out a wild shriek: "You left me all alone, a widow with two little orphans! How did they carry you to your grave? Woe is me! If not for Yurka, I'd put an end to it all."

It seemed like no one cried; there were no tears left for the little one about to be buried. Only Yurka's mother shouted in a loud, crackling voice for all to hear, "Dysentery killed my poor little baby! No medicine, no food. Could it be any worse?"

I looked up at the sky; it was pale and cloudless. A swallow twittered in the air. A lark soared up jubilantly. Suddenly, the shoemaker stopped and put down the casket on the soft, velvety grass in front of a deep, dark, open ravine in the ground. I bent over and saw the open pit, then recoiled in terror. There were flocks of ants and slimy worms crawling around. Down below, there were other little caskets piled up, one on top of the other. They were all different shapes, all different sizes, but in all of them rested the remains of little children. We all knelt around the grave.

The shoemaker jumped down into the grave, trying to fit Genka's coffin on top of the others. All at once, a fat black rat with glittering eyes jumped out of a little coffin and started a wild chase around the grave. We all ran away in horror. The deaf shoemaker heard nothing. Ignoring the rats and children, he went on as usual, pushing and pulling the caskets.

"That's where the dead children live," Yurka whispered to me, "and they play around with rats, too. We have a rat under our house. Did you see it? Even our cat is afraid of it."

"I want to go home," I cried, pleading with him. "My mother is looking for me, I am scared. We must go home before it turns dark. Don't forget that you suffer from 'chicken blindness!' When the sun goes down you cannot see a thing and I have to lead you home holding your hand. But I don't know my way home from here. We might fall into one of the open ditches and the rats will eat us up."

Everybody crossed themselves, and we left Genka's little casket down below, returning to the truck where the driver was impatiently waiting for us.

Once we approached our gray little house and I saw the light in our window, I relaxed. Quick as a squirrel, I jumped out of the truck, grabbed the trunk of our tree, and scrambled home through the window. My mother was beside herself.

"You went along to the cemetery without my permission?!" she shouted hysterically at the top of her lungs. "All day long with nothing to eat! You get skinnier by the hour, and no wonder—"

"We buried Genka," I whispered quietly, but she went on: "Little Genka was beginning to look like a bird, so thin and pale, just like you!"

I didn't listen. I sat myself down, buried in thought. Why, only a day earlier Genka had announced proudly, "Today we are rich! Very rich!"

"How rich?" we wanted to know.

"My *babushka*—my grandma—brought home two full pails of water, but we don't even know what to do with it!"

Our door always stood locked; Yurka's door was always open. From across the hall that night, we could hear the harmonica playing. There was wild laughter and dancing. Hands were clapping. There was drinking, merriment, and crying at the same time, marking the occasion of the loss of a little three-year-old boy who, just yesterday, had been so very rich.

CHAPTER 15

First Flash of Escape from Behind the Iron Curtain

$\mathcal{I}$t all began with my parents whispering something incomprehensible to each other. I sensed that they were anxious to conceal something from me. In time, I have learned that due to their wretched life they were planning an escape from the "best of all possible worlds." This time, it was a perfect opportunity, as this day saw the end of World War II.

The Red Army soldiers were visible at every bus stop, and trams were overcrowded with uniformed military men. The women in our house were in high spirits; they expected their sons and husbands back from the front. The snow outside was melting, and we kids frolicked in the front yard where the outhouse, still full of somewhat frozen excrement, stood.

A few months later, in January, I entered the second grade, and found out that the teacher, Maria Yefimovna, was the same teacher I had had in first grade. As soon as we were seated, she announced to all the new students, "If you know anybody from your first grade, you can pair up and sit next to them."

I didn't know anybody, but somebody knew me. Her name was Nadka. We lived on the same street. She was Ukrainian, neatly dressed, and confided in me that her mother worked in a munitions factory, while her father came home drunk almost every night,

36

throwing up in the same corner of their yard before entering the one room they lived in.

We soon became best friends. We never spoke about the war as long as the Germans lurked outside our city confines. Instead we spoke about food, which was scarce, and the fairy tales in the storybooks we read. I confided in her that my folks were thinking of escaping. Little did I know how dangerous this information was, once it was revealed.

We somehow managed to have potatoes and even rolls, occasionally, due to my mother's skills at bartering. She knew that the surrounding villages lacked salt, and there were no highways to deliver any food supplies to the big city where we lived. Only when the Volga River froze could the trucks travel distances.

My mother knew the wisdom of bartering at the Bazaar, exchanging an old pair of shoes for a bundle of salt. And off we went, Mother and I, to a little village across the Volga River by steamboat.

The journey took several hours, and when we arrived at the little village of "Krasno-Armeysk," a Red Army village, a breathtaking panorama unfolded before my eyes: The green hills, cows, goats wandering aimlessly through the unpaved streets, red roosters chasing white hens, and amid it all, little houses like mushrooms with red roofs, just like the fables in the storybooks. For the salt, my mother picked up milk, cheese, onions, rolls, and cucumbers.

My parents were thinking seriously of fleeing but they had one impediment: their Russian passports read that they were born in Litzmanshtadt, Germany, instead of Lodz, Poland. It seems that with Hitler's invasion of Poland, he renamed their birthplace Lodz to Litzmanshtadt and Poland to Germany. The Fuhrer was convinced that all of Europe would be part of his Third Reich.

Meanwhile, friends of my parents began returning from the slave labor camps, and some stayed with us. Their passports stated that they were Polish refugees, having escaped Poland when the Germans invaded.

Both my parents owned citizen passports, because they had crossed the Polish-Russian border in 1932 illegally. They had to invent a way to escape their beleaguered life, in spite of any hindrance, namely, in this case, Russian passports. Their scheme was simple. They would "lose" their present passports—bury them—and try to pick up new ones, hoping this time to straighten out their status.

My mother was the first one to undertake this venture. She took a calculated risk and marched off to the passport office in the dark of night. The streets were besieged by Red Army soldiers, so there was no way to get to the passport window.

At daybreak, she finally reached her destination.

The clerk cried out, "Next!"

My mother's heart pulsated wildly. There she was, her life hanging by a hair's breadth.

"Madam!" cried the clerk. "What is it you want?"

Mother could only stammer, "I – I – I need a passport!"

"Where am I going to get you a passport?" The clerk nearly choked on the sound of his own voice. "We ran out of them a fortnight ago! Don't you see the turmoil, the mayhem? Thousands of soldiers, and I'm the only clerk here. . . . All I can do for you is a temporary pass, good for only nine months. Come back in nine months, and we'll issue you a brand-new passport. All I need from you now is your name, and your city and country of birth.

Mother was delirious. The clerk handed her a temporary document stating that she had been born in Lodz, Poland. That's all she needed. Out of breath and on wings of euphoria, she reached home, where she quickly woke up my father and insisted he run helter-skelter over to the passport office in the hope of acquiring the same temporary pass.

Equipped with the temporary documents, my father took over and initiated the escape, asking help from one of their friends, Mr. Polishciuk, who was on his way back home, from the Gulag to Poland. During the war, my mother used to send packages of onions to Mr. Polishciuk in the slave labor camp in Siberia, knowing that, without them, prisoners would acquire scurvy and lose their teeth due to gum disease.

Father was determined that Mr. Polishciuk should escort my mother and me to the border town of Lwów, or Lemberg, in the Ukraine, the border town that separated Poland from Russia. Father would send us off, equipped with a document that stated that their friend Mr. Polishciuk was mentally unstable and in need of an escort.

In the meantime, both of my parents made up a code that meant, as soon as my mother and I arrived in Lwów, we were to send him a bogus telegram stating that his child was deathly ill and that he should come immediately to the rescue. Of course, that would mean that the border between Russia and Poland was open, due to the Red Army soldiers returning home. Father stayed behind in the hope of getting written permission from the head of the *Voyenstroy,* or army sup-

Author and her mother in Germany

ply depot, from which boots and military coats were expedited to the front. He needed written permission from a doctor stating that he suffered from the last stages of tuberculosis and was in need of an immediate release to get to a sanatorium for him to proceed with his plan—of course, bribery always worked wonders in obtaining such things.

CHAPTER 16

Mother and I Escape First: Lodz Landing, and What a Landing!

*T*he journey to Lemberg (Lwów) in the Ukraine took us two weeks by train. My mother took along a bundle of dried toast and a pillow for me to sleep on.

There were no facilities to relieve ourselves; everyone had to crouch under the train once it stopped. At every railroad station, hot water called *kipyatok* was available for purchase.

We arrived in Lemberg and stayed with so-called friends. Father had supplied us with their address. We settled in while my mother immediately began to send off several telegrams to Father stating I was terribly ill and that he should come and get us—meaning the Russian-Polish border was open—all to no avail; there was no reply. After several weeks, the lady of the house informed us that the police were scouring every apartment in the building to make sure that every tenant was registered with the police headquarters. We were told to leave.

That struck my mother like a thunderbolt. What to do? Go back home to search for my father, or cross the border into Poland on our own, leaving Father behind? When panic struck, Mother was unwavering and emphatic; she decided on the spot, come hell or high water, that we were leaving Russia and taking the train bound for Poland.

Within several hours, we were in Lodz, my mother's birthplace. It was a cold and dreary autumn day. Our train lurched to a stop, and suddenly we were confronted by a mob of Red Army soldiers. They descended on us through the doors and through the windows like locusts. Some of them settled on the roof of the train, but there were so many of them that my mother and I were unable to get off.

The soldiers were crowding the train cabins without regard to who got hurt. There was great commotion, pushing and pulling, luggage and bags were thrown in, then picked up. The soldiers began smoking and drinking vodka.

The train was about to return to Russia when my mother began to holler hysterically, which awakened the sleepy soldiers: "Let us out of here!" she yelled at the top of her lungs. "Let us out!" The sound reminded me of an animal on the way to slaughter.

One of the soldiers, who was busy loading his full suitcase in the overhead compartment, took pity on us. He opened the train window and shouted to the soldiers standing on the platform below. "Hey, buddy! Grab!"

Then he picked up my little mother by the coat collar and threw her out of the window. I came next; he grabbed me, shouting out to the soldiers standing along the railway tracks, "Catch!"

And out I flew. And if that wasn't enough, he also threw out my little pillow and the bundle of dried toast. And that is how we landed in Lodz, Poland, at the very end of the war.

Once again, we had an address that Father had provided us before we left. Once in the city of Lodz, we took a *droshky,* or horse and carriage, to a little house on the outskirts of the city proper. It turned out to be a small brick house inhabited by two sisters who had survived the Holocaust and returned to their parents' home. One of the sisters had been married but had lost her husband in Auschwitz. She told Mother that she began keeping company with a young man and that they were on the verge of marriage. Then her husband returned, doubling their tragedy.

Mother and I slept over one night, but our sleep was interrupted by constant noise from beneath the house, which stood on wooden beams. It seems the Polish hooligans were cutting down the beams in hopes that the house would fall and they would find gold in the rubble. There was no way that we would stay in that house, so we proceeded to a facility ready for the men, women, and children who had survived the gas chambers and the ones who had been hiding in the forest. Most of the survivors took up residence in such facilities, except for children who had been hidden by the nuns in several churches, some of whom refused to give up the newly baptized Jewish children when surviving parents or family members showed up to reclaim them.

Our new housing complex was situated on Jakuba Street 16 in Lodz. It was said that, during the war, this complex had served as the Lodz Ghetto. The place had an assemblage of dozens of beds and pillows, covered with clean sheets and blankets. There were no children around; I was the only one. Women surrounded me, patting me on the head, crying because they lost their own children. My mother shielded me from them, spitting *Tfu! Tfu! Tfu!* and constantly invoking the superstition of an evil eye.

While awaiting my father, who didn't show up, Mother was already making new plans. In one of them, she plotted to marry a Red Army soldier so as to procure a new name and passport under which we would be able to return home and look for my father.

I listened intently but didn't react; I knew that the Red Army soldier plot was just a delusion. She made daily trips to the Jewish community center, searching through the posted names of survivors looking for their relatives. She also brought home food products with a worried look on her face.

In the meantime, I was running a high fever. There were no infirmaries, medications, or doctors about. So I stayed in bed all day long, a weak ten-year-old hallucinating about my father's return. I would get up and look through the wide window, and each time I looked out, I saw Father returning to us. But that was just an illusion that disappeared when he didn't show up. Weeks passed with no word from my father. I was terribly worried. Who knew what had happened to him? Had he been imprisoned once again? How could he have disappeared without a trace, not even a word or a telegram?

By now, it was winter. Snow blanketed the yard; I saw people traipsing around aimlessly looking for something. My fever didn't let up. I once again made my daily walk over to the wide window, looking for my father, and suddenly I thought I saw him. He was dressed in a military uniform and in a furry hat, along with him I recognized my parents' friend Edgeh, who must have accompanied him, or was I once again in a delusional state? Who knows? This time I decided right there and then to run down the steps in my pajamas and test my hallucinations.

But there he was, the same father we had left. He caught sight of me, grabbed me in his arms, and covered me with his military coat. People around us began to cry; one papa had found his little girl, while they would never see their children again. . . .

We went upstairs, and my fever broke. Suddenly I felt so much better. I told him that Mother was either at the rabbi's house or at the communal house, looking for provisions or looking through the lists of survivors. Exhausted, I fell asleep, a happy sleep, and missed my parents' reunion.

The immigrant house where we stayed provided us with a dining hall, where people could bring in their own food and eat at tables. One evening, while we were eating in the dining area, suddenly my father got up with great haste, walked over to the next table, and asked the lady who occupied that seat, "Are you by any chance Rushkeh Gutterman?"

The woman turned around and shouted out, "Chaml! Is that really you? How did you recognize me after so many years?"

They embraced, and my father whispered, "I didn't recognize you, Rushkeh, but I recognized your fingers as you were opening the can of sardines. Nobody has fingers like you—long and graceful, like a pianist."

Bursting into tears, she told him, "These hands saved my life. Before I was shipped off to the slave labor camp, I studied medicine and became a doctor. The year was 1937, when I was arrested and sent off by foot, to the top of the world, to a place called *Novaya Ziemlya* (New Land). There I was incarcerated for many years, until the end of the war when the mother of the commandant in our camp became gravely ill. The commandant promised that if I saved his mother and brought her back to her former self, he would set me free. And that's how I wound up here in Lodz, my birthplace."

As I witnessed this tragic scene, I stood there stunned. How could someone recognize someone's fingers, I thought, and not the actual person? Years later, Dr. Rushka Gutterman (below) and I reestablished contact in Israel. She was married, had a son, and worked as a doctor in an Israeli hospital, saving the lives of others.

Dr. Rushke Gutterman

44

CHAPTER 17

The *"Brikha"* (Escape):
On the Run Once Again

*N*ews reached the *Shaaris Hapleyte,* the surviving remnants of the Holocaust, in 1946 that the Poles had been complicit in our destruction. Case in point, the Jedwabne massacre. The Jedwabne townspeople committed atrocities and premeditated murders in 1941, killing and burning to death more than 300 of their Jewish neighbors—men, women, children and infants—all just to get possession of their homes and belongings.

The Kielce pogrom in Poland in July 1946, right after the Holocaust, was the final straw, warning the returning Jews to vacate the hazardous Polish territories after one thousand years of Jewish life in Poland. The Kielce pogrom stood out as a symbol of the atmosphere that Jews encountered not only in Poland, but also in the Ukraine, a place that buried Jews alive in "Babi Yar." Hungarian *Niloshes*—Nazi collaborators—helped to send off most of the Hungarian Jews in 1944 to the gas chambers of Auschwitz-Birkenau, including those from the Carpathian Mountain territories where Jews had lived for hundreds of years. Romanians collaborated with the Nazis by creating a death camp called Transistria where many Romanian Jews lost their lives. In Lithuania, residents of the capitol city of Vilnius gathered families of Jews both from the city and from the surrounding little towns and villages and transported about a hundred thousand of them to the forest of Ponary (Ponar), where they were exterminated one by one with machine guns. Men, women, and children, all of them fell into a communal pit. It was told that the Ponary earth shook for weeks after, as if the earth had rejected the innocent victims. All of the Eastern European countries were saturated with Jewish blood, consumed in the continuous, noxious flames of rabid anti-Semitism.

At the end of 1945, a group of young patriots from Palestine undertook a clandestine Zionist operation, reaching the shores of Poland as well as other European countries. Our family was stuck in Lodz, Poland, which was then, and remains to this day, an extremely nationalistic, Catholic country.

The Brikha, named for the Hebrew word for "escape," was made up of brave young men on a mission to collect the surviving remnants of the Holocaust, with the idea of spiriting them out of Poland, and eventually out of Europe, and smuggling them illegally into Palestine, which was occupied by the British at that time. Ultimately, they succeeded in whisking approximately two hundred thousand Jews out of Eastern Europe and settling them temporarily in displaced persons (DP) camps in the American zone in Germany, France, and Italy.

The Brikha consisted mostly of young boys and girls who were ready to take up arms and fight for our homeland in Israel. But to our grief, entry into Palestine was illegal, so the survivors either embarked on a dangerous journey to the Promised Land or remained sealed off within the confines of the DP camps, while the politicians and diplomats negotiated the fate of the disseminated people.

The Brikha movement managed to reach the shores of Palestine undetected. Those who were caught were once again directed by the British military officers to detention camps on the island of Cyprus, where they were imprisoned once again under barbed wire until the establishment of the State of Israel in 1948.

My father decided that Poland was a mere Russian protectorate, that the Soviets were lurking around every corner, and that we had better leave that cursed earth. So we attached ourselves to the Brikha in Poland and, with their help, we crossed borders from Poland to Czechoslovakia to Austria on foot. Women and children sometimes hitched a ride on covered wagon-trucks, with instructions that, if intercepted along the way by border police, they were to insist that they were none others than Turkish nationals.

Men went mostly by foot, endangering their lives due to the Russians who, like dogcatchers, were abducting them from the streets, filling up their trucks with human cargo and sending them off to Siberia. Father knew of the Soviet means of catching innocent people and avoided this confrontation.

Once we reached the DP camp in Germany, my father, who was at this time in his late thirties, decided that Palestine was not for him; he had suffered too much in his lifetime to start all over again. Fighting another war for Jewish survival was not his idea of building a new life.

Hindenburg-Kaserne

CHAPTER 18

Hindenburg Kaserne (Military Barracks), Plus the Namesake of Our Camp

*I*n 1946, having walked for what seemed like an eternity, we finally reached the city of Ulm on the Danube River in the American zone. Our DP camp, Hindenburg Kaserne, was situated on the city's outskirts. The camp was surrounded by forests, cherry trees, velvety grasses dotted with sprouting wild mushrooms, and bunkers stacked away in the truncated mountains.

The camp was named after Paul Van Hindenburg (1847–1934), a general and field marshal in World War I and president of Germany until Hitler's rise to power. Hindenburg was also responsible for appointing Hitler as Chancellor of Germany.

The Nazi German passenger zeppelin that exploded in midair in 1937, killing 35 out of 100 passengers, was also named after Hindenburg. During the war, our camp had served as a Nazi military installation and an airplane base. Hindenburg Kaserne became a displaced persons camp right after Hitler's demise in 1945. The camp consisted of half a dozen dreary, crude, four-storied barracks and one airplane installation. During the war, Germans who worked in bunkers on the outskirts of camp lived within the confines of the military living quarters.

The city of Ulm housed an additional four Jewish DP camps,

among them Sedan Kaserne, Bleidorn Kaserne, Donau Bastion (a part of the ancient fortress), Boelcke Kaserne, and Ludendorff Kaserne. The city of Ulm was situated between Augsburg and Stuttgart. This was the same city that gave birth to the renowned physicist Dr. Albert Einstein, but, at that time, there was no trace of his ever having been their native son.

Originally, Hindenburg Kaserne was assigned to the Ukrainians and White Russian refugees, former prisoners of war and deserters from the Russian army. But with the increased flow of Jewish survivors into Ulm, the non-Jewish population was transferred to all-gentile camps, with one minor hitch: the Ukrainian camp personnel and board members of our camp stayed behind and refused to give up their former executive positions of authority.

As soon as our camp was completely occupied by the Jewish refugees, an ultimatum was issued by the new residents of our camp, addressed to the American military forces and the UNRRA (United Nations Relief and Rehabilitation Administration), stating that the Jews would not tolerate any non-Jewish supervision and were ready to assume all governing posts on their own. When UNRRA refused their demands, a hunger strike ensued. Left with no alternative, UNRRA relented, and the Ukrainian authorities were removed. An all-Jewish board of directors was installed, and the management of the camp began.

All official camp positions were filled by free elections. Lists of candidates were posted on the bulletin board, and each candidate was backed by a variety of Zionist political parties, except for one Independent ticket. Approximately 200 out of 900 camp inhabitants were affiliated with the Independent ticket, which was composed of Jewish Bundists, Communists, Trotskyites, and other malcontents. The camp director complied both with the orders from UNRRA and the Jewish Central Committee in Munich. Help came from several organizations, among them the IRO (International Refugee Organization).

The founding statute of IRO defined a displaced person (DP) as one who, as a result of acts of brutality, racism, bigotry, and atrocities by the Axis countries and their satellites, was uprooted from their homeland or permanent dwelling place; or as an individual who was forced into slave labor; or one who, as a result of religious or political discrimination, was driven out of his permanent dwelling place. Without the help of the IRO in the American zone of Germany, we would have faced great hardship trying to survive the long journey to nowhere.

There were several organizations that came to our aid, knowing full well that the refugees were helpless, homeless, and victims of a great tragedy.

Chaim Schmulewitz (Center) in Hindenburg-Kaserne

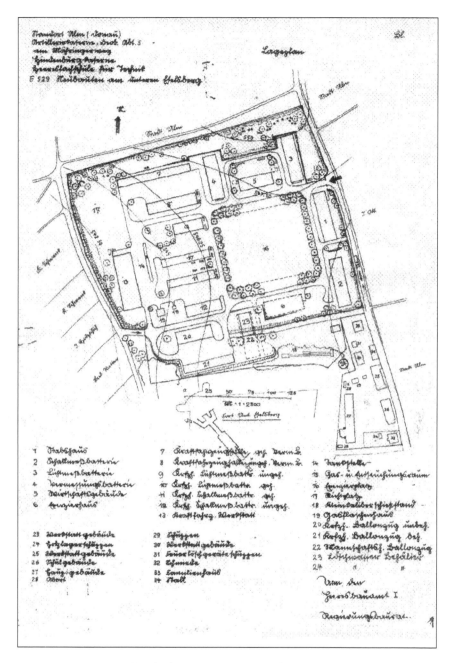

Hindenburg-Kaserne Map 1936–1938

CHAPTER 19

THE JOINT DISTRIBUTION COMMITTEE

by Chaim Schmulewitz

OUR CITY OF ULM IS BLESSED. FOR INSTANCE, WHAT WOULD the Jewish refugees have done if they had been allowed to apply only to the one board of directors? They would have probably not made it. Instead, the Lord took notice of this predicament and created a Joint committee, which was in charge in the internal affairs of each camp. You can imagine what the city committee suffered. Ulm's Joint must be having fits dealing with all of the four camps in Ulm proper.

The Joint was in charge of internal and external affairs of the camps. Jews besieged the Joint the way they used to pay visits to their rabbi. They poured out their troubles, asked for advice, requested a search for lost members of their families, and so on. There were even those who came just for curiosity's sake. A permanent visitor to the Joint was a Yiddish poet, who came daily to complain about his critics.

A tailor demanded his own sewing machine, refusing to join the camp workshop, and claimed he was a top-notch dress designer and it was below his dignity to mingle among the "riffraff." One Jew refused to fly to Paraguay, claiming it was too dangerous and the plane stood a good chance of crashing. Now that he survived such a disaster, he would not take his life into his own hands. He demanded transportation by train. Let it take another week, he was in no hurry, and above all, he must get there alive.

A young woman was in hysterics; her husband had mistreated her. A young man came about unrequited love. The Joint was like a beehive, buzzing day and night, but they were patient, knowing they were dealing with a broken society.

A zicung fun Jidiszn Lager Komitet

A meeting of the Jewish Camp Committee
(from *Ulm Album*, Chaim Schmulewitz, 3rd from left)

CHAPTER 20

One of the Many Songs
We Sang in Camp

As a young teen, I kept an album where I wrote down every song we sang in camp in four languages: Russian, Polish, Yiddish and Hebrew. Included were love songs, patriotic songs, Holocaust songs, tragic songs, and happy songs.

I also illustrated every page of my album with colorful crayons sent to us by American children in care packages. I brought the entire album with me to America in 1949. I was no doubt the only child in all of the DP camps after the war that not only kept a record of every song we sang, but managed to bring those songs to America. Today, a copy of my album, with its songs and drawings, is located and stored in the U.S. Holocaust Memorial Museum in Washington, D.C.

Among the eighty songs I chose to translate from the Yiddish is a song that dealt with corruption and dishonesty during those years among the adults. One must remember, these refugees—who had survived the Nazi affliction of the Holocaust, the Russian barter system and black-marketeering, the Ukrainian Babi-Yar pogrom, the Polish extortions, and betrayal—trusted *nobody*. Now, confronted with the lack of delivery of goods for the camp population, they sang:

"Ten Wagon Trains from UNRRA"
(United Nations Relief and Rehabilitation Administration)

Ten wagon trains from UNRRA,
Laden for us in a line,
The night was slightly dark—
All that remained were nine.

Nine wagon trains from UNRRA,
Hoping it won't come late,
One veered off to the left,
All that remained were eight.

Eight wagon trains from UNRRA,
Sent to us from heaven—
There was a bitter winter,
All that remained were seven.

Seven wagon trains from UNRRA,
With clothing, coffee, a mix,
While crossing a dark forest,
All that remained were six.

Six wagon trains from UNRRA,
Coming from Argentina Drive.
One of them got lost;
All that remained were five.

Five wagon trains from UNRRA,
With wine from door to door.
An accident occurred.
All that remained were four.

Four wagon trains from UNRRA,
With toddler toys that were free,
Avoiding a long, dark tunnel.
All that remained were three.

Three wagon trains from UNRRA
A bridge it couldn't get through.
The trains veered to the right.
All that remained were two.

Two wagon trains from UNRRA
Thought that they were done,
They tried to reach us faster.
All that remained was one.

One wagon train from UNRRA
We all expected plenty,
We opened the doors all excited,
It turned out to be empty.

The camp crowd sang this song to accuse the board of directors of dishonesty and corruption.

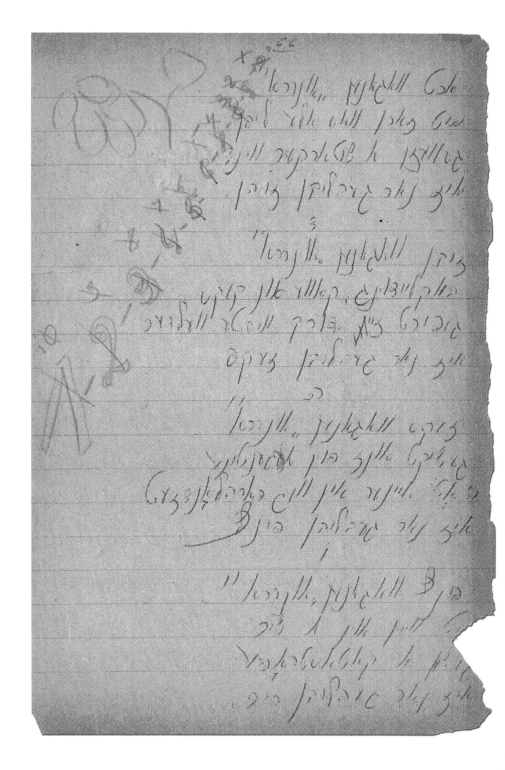

Yiddish Song: "10 Wagons from UNWRRA" from Author's Journal

Уходили с берега. Катюша
Ухдыила с берега. домой с

Конец

CHAPTER 21

Board of Directors
in Hindenburg Kaserne

The newly formed board of directors was made responsible for the just and honest distribution of food, shelter, heating, clothing, medical assistance, education, and cultural activities. They also kept books of produce and merchandise circulating in camp and conducted daily meetings.

The administration was subdivided into various departments, among them the Employment Office, the Welfare Department, the Commerce and Finance Department, the Department of Housing, the Office of Religious Affairs, and the Department of Cultural Affairs. Every camp, including ours, maintained a Historical Society in charge of gathering firsthand information of Nazi atrocities against the Jews. There was also a Medical Board and a board of Professional Dress Designers. In addition, the AJDC (the American Joint Distribution Committee) sponsored ORT, a series of vocation and training programs. ORT teachers and pupils were entitled to special rations according to an established schedule.

Everyone had to work to earn their food and clothing. The wage distribution system was categorized as follows: Wages for the employed were distributed per a point system that earned food supplies and other articles. Food was allotted based on the minimum calorie requirements. Wages and the welfare support were decided by JOINT and the Central Committee in Munich. Uniform wages and the standards of welfare cases for the entire zone were established, including a bookkeeping system with central accounting control. A centralized supply security system served the entire zone. The new supply system was divided into two categories: one served the welfare recipients and reimbursed wages for the established categories, and the second included a system of documentation, bookkeeping, and accounting.

Among the assortment of jobs available, board members were the highest paid. Those employed directly by the local boards were in charge of housing and the distribution of food, clothing, and coal. There was great commotion, anger, and reproach directed at the staff of the board of directors with each apportionment of food supplies or allotment of clothing. The members of the board were addressed as "robbers" and "murderers" by the refugees, as the good garments were nowhere in sight; there were only hand-me-downs.

A welfare system oversaw the care of invalids, ORT students, the sick, children ages one through seventeen, persons over fifty-five, and pregnant women. Hospital recovery patients and penal institutions were all part of the system. Most of the refugees were decent, upstanding folk, bewildered, orphaned, and deeply—very deeply—injured and distressed human beings.

There were those who loved to mingle in our camp and spread false rumors. These rumors would throw the camp population into a spin, causing a split into pro and con groups with regard to the issues discussed. All this resulted in screams and shouts

Der Inwalidn-Farband

The Invalid Committee (from *Ulm Album*)

until the mailman showed up. Everyone expected a letter or care package from America. The Jews were hungry for a sensational piece of news, and God didn't forsake.

On a sunny day, the camp would fill up with baby carriages and proud mothers. The DP camps had the highest birth rate in the world at that time. Everyone was aware of his neighbor's affairs, except for the Hungarians, who spoke primarily among themselves. They didn't mingle with the rest of the crowd; they took separate walks, and sat apart from the Polish, Galician, and Lithuanian Jews as if to say, "They are not of our ilk." The rest of the camp population considered their neighbors to be like their own family; they were related and united by tragedy. Every one of them had lost their world, their closest family members and relatives. Away from politics, they treated each other with kid gloves.

Neighbors would share their tragedies, their frustrations, their losses, and their heartaches, cursing the gentiles among whom they had lived all of their lives, but most of all they poured their wrath at the world that had stood idly by and done nothing.

In Gan Jeladim

In the Kindergarten (from *Ulm Album*)

CHAPTER 22

The Underworld Culture

A sizable underworld culture flourished in Hindenburg Kaserne, consisting of the strong-fisted Jewish underworld characters who had spent their prewar years as reckless youths in big cities of Poland, Romania, and Hungary. They were good at survival skills. Trading on the black market inside the camp went undisturbed; merchandise was brought in from the outside, be it clothing, vegetables, meat, gold rings, watches, blankets, dresses, and all sorts of articles the camp was lacking. This was considered illegal, and the UNRRA officials objected to it. Nevertheless, they paid little heed to its existence.

There were those in camp who specialized in black marketeering, counterfeit money, and the smuggling of illegal human cargo across the borders to France and Austria. If they were caught outside the confines of camp, the German judicial system was reluctant to give them stiff sentences. They were released on the condition they leave immediately on the illegal immigration to Palestine (*Aliya*).

Rogzhe (Doormat) was the nickname of an underworld family named Alba. They had two daughters, one of whom took me aside and confided in me the experience of her weekends. They were picked up in a limousine, which already had a few passengers, all of whom had paid exorbitant smuggling fees to their parents. The sisters accompanied these refugees, desperate to cross the border, as the limousine dropped them off in a remote location.

61

The girls led the way that they were taught, through the forests and the hills, to the nearest clandestine border crossing. Once the "mission" was accomplished, they returned to where the limousine was waiting, returning them to our camp. Their biggest complaint was that their parents didn't share the "bounty" with them.

Chaim Schmulewitz (left) with Refugee

Chaim Schmulewitz (top) with Refugees

CHAPTER 23

THE UNDERWORLD IN OUR CAMP

by Chaim Schmulewitz

THERE WERE A NUMBER OF UNDERWORLD CHARACTERS IN our camp, survivors of the famed *"Warshever Untervelt"* (Warsaw Underworld); others stemmed from Lodz, and still others from Romania and Hungary. An assortment of crooks and smugglers formed a kinship among them, but never disturbed the camp population in any way.

They did their work on the outside, picking pockets, hit men, bank robbers, and smugglers, engaged in crossing illegal aliens into France and other European countries. They also dealt in counterfeit money. As acting chief of police of our camp in 1948 and 1949, I described the following incident:

"Upon learning of a hot counterfeit operation in progress, I called in two suspects, well-known underworld figures, dealers in counterfeit money. I gave them ample warning to stop spreading the stuff among camp residents or be ready for a prison term.

"They disregarded my warning and proceeded with their business as usual. Having informers among them, I found out they were due to arrive in camp at midnight with the stuff on them, accompanied by a *fraulein*—a young German woman. All three were detained and searched. As the counterfeit dollars materialized, I summoned the MP (Military Police), and they, in turn, escorted the threesome out of camp and into the German detention center in town. But Jewish prisoners in German jails had an easy time of it. They appealed to the "Brikha," the organization in charge of smuggling illegal Jews to Palestine, and they were promptly bailed out."

CHAPTER 24

We the Children—Schooling

*A*mong the close to one thousand Jews in our camp, a third of them were children of assorted ages, and though we were not ripe in years, we already carried a heavy burden on our youthful shoulders. The most worrisome problem was that the war had robbed us not only of our normal youth, but also of our formal education.

Opposite the camp stretched a small, dense forest where we children picked cherries, berries, and mushrooms during the summer months. A favorite game of ours consisted of catching bumblebees, attaching a thread around their tail, and pretending they were kites. Sometimes, my father and I used to walk outside our camp toward a cave in the mountain. Inside, we found a great number of crumpled shoes strewn on one side of the bunker, while on the opposite side we found rusted airplane parts and crumbly, discarded tanks. Father told me these were the residues of the war.

Occasionally, we children contrived a trip to the city of Ulm proper so we could watch a foreign film. One German musical stuck in my mind, especially the name of the actress, Marika Rökk, who sang and danced and made me so very happy for a while. Much later, when my family and I traveled in Switzerland, there she was, not on the screen but on stage, still singing and dancing. I discovered then that she was miniature in stature, not at all as she appeared in the German films.

In wintertime, we youngsters exited the camp's grounds and went sledding down the thickly snow-carpeted mountain peak on wooden planks. As we frolicked around the mountainside, we were filled with amazement at the sight of the little houses surrounded by white picket fences where the Germans lived. We had only seen such houses in storybooks. In the spring and summer, their windows were adorned with colorful flowerpots, which made us children all the more resentful of them.

Their homes were embellished with gardens bursting into a multicolored panorama of ornate flowers in bloom. We brewed envy and hatred toward those peaceful little German homes, resting so dreamily and free from care on the mountainside. Nothing would do but for us to pull off a prank out of envy. Stealthily we would open the front gates, ring their doorbells twice, and speedily flee, observing over our shoulders as we ran, the Germans pursuing us with angry curses and clenched fists. All the way down the road, we could hear the Germans

Author (Top row, 1st on right) in Classroom

shouting after us: *"Verfluchte Jüdisch Donnerwetter!"* (Damn Jewish thunderstorms!) Oh! But how we enjoyed our little prank and the childish revenge. For us it was a joyful occasion.

Do not forget that we children lived in a DP camp, in military barracks, isolated from the world around us, with two families to a room. In winters, we were freezing; in summers, we were bathed in our own sweat. And here we came across so much beauty, not to mention the dreamy little houses, the homes of the people who were guilty for our sorrow.

I made several friends in camp. My best friend was an unhappy and morose child. She used to complain that her father suffered daily from migraine headaches and that her stepmother didn't treat her well but was a loving mother to her own son. She constantly threatened to commit suicide by jumping from her second-floor window. I used to comfort her until she calmed down. This became a daily routine when we were ten and eleven years old.

On the other hand, I had a friend who was a happy-go-lucky little blond girl, bursting with laughter at any occasion, always on the go. Equipped with a colorful little blanket in hand, she would run around the camp looking for a tree to climb on. The boys followed her like little puppies, trying to climb on the very tree she sat on, enticing them to catch her.

We children had no books and no toys, and we never saw a radio, a television, or a telephone. We didn't even know that such things existed. Our entertainment consisted of singing, dancing, and retelling stories based on the films we had seen in town or the books we had read. We had a tough time adjusting to camp life, but especially to the new school with a new language. My class consisted of children of all ages, many of them undisciplined and with little education due to the loss of the war years.

Chaim Schmulewitz (Top row, right) in Classroom

As soon as we settled into Hindenburg Kaserne, the camp erected a kindergarten, but the elementary and middle school for all three DP camps was situated in the Sedan Kaserne and Neu Ulm camps. We children were picked up each morning by open trucks, no matter the weather, and returned home in the late afternoon.

The prewar Jewish teachers had a poor command of the Hebrew language. This put great pressure on the children, whose education had been interrupted by the war years. Some of the children experienced great difficulty, even in simple subjects. In fact, many times the students would react violently to the unfamiliar terminology—in this case, Modern Hebrew—creating teacher-student hostilities.

The curriculum consisted of the following subjects: Hebrew, arithmetic, Bible, nature, geography, history, art, singing, and gymnastics. All the subjects were taught in Modern Hebrew, with the Sephardic pronunciation, or would have been if not for the fact that most of our teachers were familiar with the old biblical, sacred tongue, in the Ashkenazi pronunciation. It must have been that, in their youth, the teachers had trained with a *rebbe* (rabbinic teacher) either in a *Kheyder* (a religious school for very young boys) or in *Yeshivas* (religious academies for older boys). The only ones who came prepared linguistically, speaking Hebrew, were those who were sent from Palestine to organize Zionist schools and those with political party affiliations, be it to the left, center, or right. The trouble was that none of us

had ever heard of or spoken Hebrew, and the same was true for our parents; very few of them spoke the ancient vernacular of the Bible.

As each new day dawned in camp, the children in the upper grades were

Author (2nd row, 4th from right) in Classroom

gathered alongside the camp gates, waiting for the pick-up trucks. Our school was located in Boelcke-Kaserne. These schools served all the Jewish children in Ulm, where we were indoctrinated in the spirit of Political Zionism, a political movement for the establishment and support of a national homeland for Jews in Palestine.

The camp housed a small lending library. Some of the teachers were still unable to transmit their subject in Modern Hebrew, especially our geography instructor, Mr. Shtern. He kept repeating the same Hebrew word throughout the hour—*"Eyfo? Eyfo? Eyfo?"*—meaning, "Where? Where? Where?" and sprang it on me, calling out "Miriam! *Eyfo Madagaskar!*" I, for one, had never heard of such a place, let alone made myself familiar with the world map that hung on the wall.

And, if that wasn't enough, we were forbidden to communicate in Yiddish among ourselves anywhere in the camps; we had to speak only Hebrew, despite that it was a language we didn't know. As a matter of fact, the *shlikhim* (those who came on a mission from Palestine) founded our secular Hebrew School called *"Bet Sefer Tarbut,"* the School of Culture. No culture was actually taught in this school, if we knew what culture even meant. The teachers who also lacked the knowledge of the ancient tongue threatened us: if they caught one of us speaking Yiddish, we would be punished. Of course, that never came to fruition. At first, we were a bit reluctant to continue speaking Yiddish to each other, not knowing what kind of punishment would be doled out. As time passed, we forgot all about their threats and proceeded to live out our private lives in Yiddish.

Author (3rd row, 7th from right) in Classroom

CHAPTER 25

Esslingen: A Paradise for Us Children

The AJDC (American Jewish Distribution Committee), the Joint, and the camp's medical department cosponsored adequate medical and nursing services for the children. The younger ones were offered a two-week retreat in the town of Esslingen, Germany, every summer. One summer, I was one of the lucky ones to be picked to go to this sprawling garden estate. The staff chosen for the summer-camp administration was drawn from a pool of trainees and nurses that had been sent by the AJDC Recreation Department.

During this retreat, from time to time, we were taken to the Salzburg Music Festival and introduced to cultural events. The main event of the day was to observe the city's cuckoo clock that entertained us with the figurines that kept coming out from little doors, singing and dancing every hour on the hour to a German tune. There was music all around us. We also participated in discussions, but foremost in my mind was the healthy environment with its peace and quiet and joy. We were also treated to an imaginary radio show in which we had to perform. Of course, I was very bashful, but I did it, together with friends I acquired in Esslingen, both boys and girls my age.

And, to top it off, we were served wonderful meals we had neither seen nor tasted before. For breakfast, we had farina sprinkled with chocolate chips; for lunch, an assortment of soups, fruit cups, and marzipan; and, for dinner, roasted pigeons stuffed with rice and raisins.

We girls were assigned separate rooms from the boys. One night, when it was time for bed, we girls jumped onto the beds and, instead of mattresses, we found ourselves in puddles of water. It seems that the boys played a prank on us. They had lowered our mattresses and placed buckets full of water on top of them.

A week later, we girls, equipped with black shoe paste, string, and toothpaste, waited until midnight to make sure that the boys were fast asleep. We crawled into their room, tied their feet to the beds, spread toothpaste on their faces, and covered their slippers with the shoe paste, and so the deed was done. We choked with laughter as we crawled back to our room. In the morning, we heard the boys yelling and screaming, "Untie us!" Once they were free, they stepped into their slippers and began slipping and sliding.

A week later we paired up, girlfriends and boyfriends. My new friend Rifka introduced me to a redheaded twelve-year-old boy named Yitzchok who wanted to kiss me. He told me he had a trick way of doing it.

"What is your trick?" I wanted to know.

He put the palm of his hand on my cheek and kissed his own hand.

What wonderful moments and memories!

Author in summer camp, Esslingen, Germany

CHAPTER 26

OUR REFUGEE CAMP, HINDENBURG KASERNE

by Chaim Schmulewitz

I AM A HINDENBURGER PATRIOT, A BONA-FIDE FLESH-AND-blood Hindenburger. I have been here since its inception. Although Hindenburg is much younger than the other camps in Germany, it is more renowned. Ulm, with its four Jewish Camps, has earned the esteem of all the Jewish DP camps: we provide entertainment, and the Repertoire Theater groups all clamor to come to Ulm with its four populous camps.

Hindenburg is surrounded with forests and orchards. Once upon a time, Jews would have driven miles for fresh air. Every blade of grass, every tree, would have been looked upon as a summer home, but today, Jews have other things than summer homes on their agenda.

Hindenburg is teeming with life. There is nothing that cannot be found in this camp of mine. The entire world is here. I sincerely doubt whether New York has so much to offer. Take, for instance, the multitude of political parties. Can New York really compete with Hindenburg Kaserne? I doubt it. Should a split occur in one party, Hindenburg would awaken with an additional one.

Hindenburg organized an Israeli recruiting and immigration center called *Aliya,* a committee of the Israel Defense Ministry, which encouraged donations. There was a *Bikur Khoylim,* a group that visits the sick at home and in the hospital; a *Khevre-Kadishe,* or burial society; and a *Hakhnoses Kale*—an orphaned bride's fund. We had not, up until then, married off one of our own.

We have a House of Study, a *Talmud Toyre* (religious school), a Committee of Religion, a *Khazn* (cantor) a *Shoykhet* (ritual slaughterer), a sexton, a Sabbath Observers Society as well as old Jewish-style wedding epigrammatist, a *Badkhn*.

There is also a kindergarten, a library with Yiddish and Hebrew books, a Historical Society, a theater with local actors and actresses, including an artistic director, a choir and a conductor, a sports club, a bulletin board newsletter, our own Court of Justice, and a radio announcer. I am ready to wager that there is a greater officialdom here than in the Kingdom of Luxembourg, with a plethora of departments, such as cultural, housing, food, clothing, work, a veritable government, and a police force with its own Chief of Police. Me.

As far as professionals go, we have tailors, shoemakers, an ORT School for vocational training, locksmiths, mechanics, linen seamstresses, dressmakers, welders, and others. There is also an ambulatory with qualified and semi-qualified doctors.

Hindenburgers were also on the Exodus (the illegal boat to Palestine), and in the internment camps in Cyprus thanks to the British, who saw the Jews as Polish nationals and wanted them to be deported to their homeland, Poland. They followed British orders that prevented the Jews from reaching Palestine.

People in camp didn't address each other by their proper names; they used nicknames or mocking names. This phenomenon became a custom in our camp. Among these nicknames were "Chamberlain," "The Greasy Lamp-Post," "The Little Ox," "Moishe Dandik," "Bevin," and "The Frozen One."

Meet "Purim-Peysakh," the Fire Marshal. He was a middle-aged man, a former forest merchant from Lithuania, who had suffered through Hitler's hell, and now he was one of us. Purim-Peysakh didn't waste much time. All at once he became a porter, worked himself up to a plain laborer, a policeman, and finally made it to fire marshal.

He loved to ridicule and jest; he was even a rhyme-master. Convinced that he was the first Jewish fire marshal since the destruction of the Second Temple in Jerusalem, he knew and told of several marshals, among them Marshal Stalin, Marshal Chiang Kai Shek, Marshal Tito, and of course he was well acquainted with the Marshall Plan. Purim-Peysakh also performed fire drills and lectured on the history of fires since the beginning of time, until his own position as Fire-Marshall in Hindenburg Kaserne.

On the other hand, we had "The Greasy Lamp-Post." He came from a small town near Warsaw. A former Yeshivah student, a child of a well-to-do family, he made it from Stalingrad to Berlin, was wounded several times and decorated for bravery, and now he was a displaced person. Upon arrival to Hindenburg Kaserne, he joined the police force. As soon as he got his helmet and nightstick, he was on guard against freedom fighters from the east, namely the communists.

All day long he sat in the police precinct and argued, "Did it really pay to carry on this Greasy War, where over thirty million Lampposts lost their lives, and now, three years later, the Greasy Diplomats are brewing up a new slaughterhouse that will put to shame all the other Greasy Wars? And the stupid Lampposts are being cut down like hay! We are mum about the whole Greasy deal, as if they don't mean us! They sit around in their villas, surrounded by Greasy watchdogs, and cook up new plans to eliminate us. As sure as my name is Greasy Lamppost, I am sure that they built for themselves shelters, where the Greasy, lousy cholera wouldn't even get them! And as long as we are willing to be Lampposts, they are willing to be Greasy little Big Shots."

Rashke was a woman whose voice was on display all day long in camp. She used to accost anyone who would listen. "I am for mankind," she would holler with her hands in the air. "I am ready to sacrifice my life for mankind. My past is forgotten. Today I am a respectable, married woman and my husband supports me."

Despite her three little ones, Rashke held the position of "Sanitar" in charge of sanitary efficiency, and if she caught someone in the act of polluting, that person was not to be envied. She dismissed all the German maids from camp. She had one message for the mobsters in camp: "I will bury you yet, because I am for mankind."

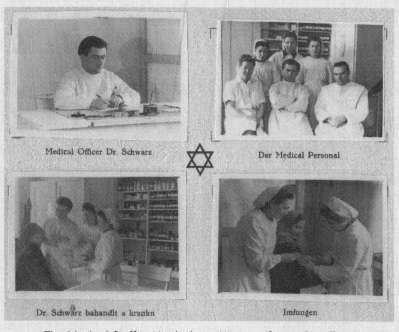

Medical Officer Dr. Schwarz

Der Medical Personal

Dr. Schwarz bahandlt a krankn

Imfungen

The Medical Staff in Hindenburg-Kaserne (from *Ulm Album*)

CHAPTER 27

JEWS! I NEED ADVICE ON ALL THESE POLITICAL PARTIES (A SATIRICAL ESSAY)

by Chaim Schmulewitz

I HAVE—PRAISE THE LORD—A WIFE, YENTE-PESHE, AND FIVE children. No evil eye should befall them! That's good. What's good? Actually, not so good!

From dawn to late at night, ours is a madhouse. My oldest son, Moyshe, is a right Poale-Zion Zionist. The second son, Gedalye, is a left Poale-Zion Zionist. The third one, Avrum, is Hitakhdut United. Sorele is a Revisionist, Beytar Zev Zhabotinsky's tribe Zionist. My youngest, Mirele, is a Shomer Hatsayir, an all-the way to the left Zionist. My wife, Yente Peshe, is an Independent, and I split myself three ways: I was a Mizrahi Zionist, then I joined Aguda, and then I split again and became Brit-Yeshurun.

I help my Sorele shout, "Both banks of the Jordan!"

Each morning, as soon as they open their eyes, it begins. "Khaluke!" "Division!" "No division!"

Mirele shouts, "A Jewish-Arab State!"

My Yente-Peshe hollers loudest of them all, "Shut your mouths! God in heaven!"

I didn't sleep an entire week. My son Avrum of the Poaley Zion (Jewish Labor Party) split off, so my son Moyshe of the Poaley-Zion Hitakhdut (United) and my son Gedalye of Poaley Zion to the left started working on Avrum. Moyshe took him aside and started pulling him to the right and Gedalye to the left.

Suddenly Avrum lets everybody know. "Nothing doing! I am organizing a new political party, and I am calling it 'Yikhud' (Together)!"

You hear, people, that I lived through all this? I must be made from iron. My Yente-Peshe is already in bed for a week. Last week I felt better. It was quiet in the house, so I thought to myself, *Messiah has arrived. Maybe my political parties united?*

I live in a DP camp in Ulm, and in Ulm, the Arabs in town have been hitting Jews in the streets, so a miracle occurred. My Shomer-Hatsayir (Guardian of the Young—Socialist Party), and the Revisionist, and the left Poaley-Zion with the Brit Yeshurun, and my Independent wife, and my new party all united, getting ready to fight back. My house turned as quiet as the reading room in a library. Everyone behaved as civilized people. I knew it—from then on, we were going to have peace. But something went wrong. As soon as it got quiet with the Arabs, my house turned into hell again. Help me! Give me advice! How do I live through all this?

Vice-Prezes fun Lagerkomitet Ch. Szmulewicz

Chaim Schmulewitz, Vice President of Camp Board (from *Ulm Album*)

CHAPTER 28

Once Again Confronting Anti-Semitism, Right After the Holocaust

$\mathcal{J}$ews and anti-Semitism could be compared to Siamese twins attached at the head. It is not an easy task to separate them. There was never an era in Jewish history that was exempt from this dreadful disease. The true face of Jew-hatred hides under a variety of masks, sitting in ambush behind a veil of prejudice and racism, ready to ambush.

Right after the war, the Jews were confronted by General Patton who was responsible for the Jewish DPs. The U.S. Third Army controlled part of the American-occupied zone in Germany. Its commanding officer, General George S. Patton, held strong opinions about Jewish displaced persons that were, no doubt, shared by other Americans at the same time. He wrote the following in his diary:

Late yesterday afternoon I was notified that General Eisenhower is about to arrive . . . I found out later that the purpose of his visit was to inspect the D.P. camps, particularly at least one occupied by Jews, to determine the condition of these Jews in order that he may write a letter to President Truman.

Harkins and I went to greet General Eisenhower in spite of the fact he had suggested that I not put myself out . . . While waiting, I talked to Brigadier General Mickelsen who is G-5 for Eisenhower's headquarters (in charge of D.P. affairs), and he showed me a letter from President Truman to General Eisenhower which was unnecessarily harsh and in much less considerate language than I would have used in cussing out a 2nd Lieutenant.

In 1945, Mickelsen also showed me the report of a man named Earl G. Harrison (which was enclosed in the President's letter) on the condition of Displaced Persons in Europe, particularly Jews. Harrison is a member of the State Department, dean of the Law-School at the University of Pennsylvania. He was also the representative of the Intergovernmental Committee on Refugees. The report contained many allegations against General Eisenhower and the Army, including various commanders. One of the chief complaints is that the D.P.'s are kept under guard. Of course, Harrison is ignorant of the fact that if they were not kept under guard, they would not stay in the camps, but spread all over the country like locusts, and would eventually have to be rounded up after quite a few of them had been shot and as well as a few of the Germans had murdered and pillaged.

The brilliant Mr. Harrison further objected to the sanitary conditions, again being ignorant of the fact that we frequently must use force to prevent the inmates, Germans, Jews and other people from defecating on the floor when ample facilities are provided outside.

Evidently, he wrote, the virus started by Morgenthau and Baruch both of Semitic revenge tactics against all Germans. Harrison and his associates indicate that they feel German civilians should be removed from houses for housing Displaced Persons.

There are two errors in this assumption. First, when we remove an individual German, we punish an individual German while the punishment is not intended for the individual but for the race. Furthermore, it is against my Anglo-Saxon conscience to remove a person from a house, which is a punishment, without due process of law.

In the second place, Harrison and his ilk believe that the Displaced Persons are human beings, which they are not, and this applies particularly to the Jews who are lower than animals.

I remember once at Troina in Sicily, General Gay said that it wasn't a question of the people living with the dirty animals but of the animals living with the dirty people. At that time, he had never seen a Displaced Person. Furthermore, I do not see why Jews should be treated any better or any worse than Catholics, Protestants, Mohammedans or Mormons. However, it seems apparent that we should do this, and I am going to do it as painlessly as possible, by taking a certain group of buildings in several cities and placing the Jews who do not exceed 20,000 in sort of improved ghettos.

To put the Jews on farms would be disastrous because it would break up the agricultural economy of Bavaria on which we depend for providing what food is provided which is not paid for by American taxpayers . . . If the people in Washington would stop trying to find fault with others and wake up to the extent of making the Russians take back the Poles and other people whom they have not permitted to return, the situation in Displaced Persons would be much ameliorated . . . It seems to be quite a hell of a mess.

. . . Eisenhower and I drove to Munich where we inspected a Baltic Displaced Persons camp. The Baltic people are the best of the Displaced Persons and the camp was extremely clean in all respects . . . We drove for about 45 minutes to a Jewish camp . . . established in what had been a German hospital, the buildings were therefore in a good state of repair. When the Jews arrived, they were in a bad state of repair, because the Jewish D.P.'s or at least most of them, have no sense of human relationships. They decline, where practicable to use latrines, preferring to relieve themselves on the floor.

This happened to be the Feast of Yom-Kippur, so they were all collected in a large wooden building which they called synagogue. It behooved General Eisenhower to make a speech to them. We entered the synagogue which was packed with the greatest stinking bunch of humanity I have ever seen. When we got about half way up, the head rabbi, who was dressed in a fur hat similar to that worn by Henry VIII of England and in a surplus heavily embroidered and very filthy coat, came down to meet the General.

Also a copy of the Talmud, I think it is called, written on a sheet and rolled around a stick, was carried by one of the attending physicians. First, a Jewish civilian made a very long speech which nobody seemed inclined to translate. Then General Eisenhower mounted the platform and I went up behind him, and he made a short and excellent speech, which was translated paragraph by paragraph.

However, the smell was so terrible that I almost fainted and actually about three hours later lost my lunch as the result of remembering it. General Louis Craig came to see me this morning to explain how he had arranged for taking care of the Jews.

It has been necessary for him, against his and my instincts to move twenty-two rich German families from their houses to put the animals in them. I told Craig to take pictures of the houses before they were occupied by Jews. I also told him to move the Germans with as much consideration as possible and to give them transportation to move as much of their decent property out as they could. Craig told me he had inspected another Jewish camp yesterday in which he found men and women using adjacent toilets which were not covered in any way although screens were available to make the toilets individually isolated, which the Jews were too lazy to put up.

He said the conditions and filth were unspeakable. In one room, he found ten people, six men and four women, occupying four double beds. Either the Displaced Persons never had any sense of decency or else they lost it all during their period of internment by the Germans. My personal opinion is that no people could have sunk to the level of degradation these have reached in the short space of four years.

President Harry S. Truman urged the British to allow more Jews into Palestine. But Prime Minister Attlee refused his proposal.

Both England and the U.S. were not prepared to open their borders, due to the prejudice and hatred of the Jews.

Members of the American Congress and State Department, were not capable of understanding why the refugees did not return to their homelands after the war.

Harry S. Truman has written to Congress pleading with them that this is an exceptional case, dealing with a humanitarian issue, not to forget that these are fellow human beings . . . to no avail.

—From *The Patton Papers,* Martin Blumenson

In my research at the YIVO Institute for Jewish Research, I dug up dozens of those letters and articles dealing with this scourge we call anti-Semitism. One of the letters read:

Report - dated 2/6–12, 1946
Received from AROLSEN, Germany
Subject: Riots and Orientation Programs at the Jewish D.P. camp of Lampertheim, Germany, February 6–12, 1946

On Wednesday, February 6, 1946 at about 8 p.m. I arrived at the Jewish D.P. camp of Lampertheim (near Manheim) for the purpose of leaving Jewish newspapers for the library. I found the camp and the members of U.N.R.R.A. team in a state of great agitation, dejection and excitement. Upon questioning them I discovered that the camp had experienced a small-scale riot during that afternoon.

At about 2:30 p.m. that day, a German woman had come to her house now occupied by Jews and asked a 16 year old Jewish boy to allow her to enter her former home and remove some bottles.

The Jewish boy allowed her to come in. What happened immediately thereafter is not quite clear; it is alleged that the German woman said something to the effect that if they had only burned more Jews in the gas chambers then there would be no Jews in Lampertheim.

A fight ensued. More Germans came in as did more Jews. German police (despite military regulations to the contrary) also came into the picture, some belonging to the local military detachment, passed by and saw the fight.

They called up headquarters and soon armed American soldiers rolled into the streets of the D.P. settlement on half-tracks. Shots were fired. All Jews were ordered to remain behind closed doors. Germans, on the other hand, were allowed to move freely through the streets and many of them gathered to see the G.I.'s who were rounding up the Jews.

Flipping further through the same document to page 2, I came across this incident:

. . . At about 10 p.m. I sent my assistant, Francis Bibo, on an errand through the streets of Lampertheim. He wore the regulation E.M. uniform, with the UNRRA shoulder patch, driving a duly registered former Red Cross ambulance, and was in possession of duly authorized travel orders.

He was stopped on the street by a G.I., who was also accompanied by two German policemen. The first question the American soldier asked Bibo was: *"Sind Sie Judish?"* (Are you Jewish?) This of course is not the proper sort of question to be asked. The first question to be asked is concerning travel orders, trip tickets or other identification papers authorizing travel. Bibo therefore looked at the soldier with surprise and said, "What kind of business is this? Do you want to see my orders?"

"Are you a G.I.?," asked the soldier. "What are you anyway?"

"U.N.N.R.A." answered Bibo.

"Oh, that f————n organization," replied the G.I. "You better get the hell off the street in fifteen minutes!"

"I am not subject to curfew," countered Bibo, "and I shall remain on the street as long as my duty calls for it."

"You better get the hell off the street," shouted the soldier, as Bibo rode away . . .

On Wednesday, February 6, 1946 at about 8 p.m. I arrived at the Jewish D.P. camp of Lampertheim (near Mannheim) for the purpose of leaving Jewish newspapers for the library. It seems that right after the war, some incidents between the G.I.'s and the Jews were deteriorating as G.I.'s had entered Jewish homes while drunk and assaulted and intimidated the Jews.

Incidents at Neu-Ulm

This anti-Semitic incident took place in Ludendorff Kaserne on December 8, 1947:

On the 7th of December 1947, between the hours of 11-11:30, Blass Jakob, DP Identity 470676, born 25 of September, 1904, in Poland (Jewish), was attacked by 2025 Turks or Arabs. They all were in possession of knives, but did beat him up and kicked him while he was down on the ground.

The medical report as here attached by Dr. Zlotkin, indicates that while Blass is severely beaten and wounded in many places, his condition is not critically serious. He is confined to the camp infirmary at Ludendorff Kaserne. The incident happened at the German Mail Office in Ulm. At the approach of the German Police, as Arabs or Turks ran away and the German Police brought Blass to the camp.

On Saturday evening, December 6, 1947, between the hours of 8 and 10:30 p.m., Mordke Nay, D.P. Identification #556972, born 5 January 1920, in Poland (Jewish), was found seriously wounded, about 200 meters from Ludendorff Kaserne. He was brought to the Infirmary of the Kaserne on a stretcher.

First Aid was administered to him by Dr. Zlotkin, D.P. Chief Doctor, and then he was transferred to the I.R.O. Section of the Ulm City Hospital.

According to the signed statement by Nay Mordko on December 6, between the hours of 8 and 10:30, returning from Donau Bastion (another D.P. camp in Ulm), to Ludendorff Kaserne, Neu Ulm, he was attacked by five or six dark complectioned Turks. They greeted him in Polish "Good evening!" and asked him if he was a Jew, and immediately proceeded to beat him up. Nay, thinking that they were after his money, wanted to give it to them, but they replied that they didn't want any money, because he is a Jew they must cut off his head, for the Jews in Palestine are taking away the Arab land. They knifed and beat him. In the meantime, he started to run away from them and landed in an isolated part of the woods near the camp. He managed to cry for help and a German on a bicycle called for additional help. A German woman immediately notified the camp police and the camp committee.

An interview with Mr. Nay by the I.R.O. camp director, Mr. Kats of Lindendorf Kaserne and by Jean Greenwald of A.J.D.C., on Monday, December 8th at about 1 p.m. confirms the contents in the attached statements and also the foregoing facts. The interview with the Dr., the Chief Physician of the Hospital, confirmed Nay's very critical condition.

On Saturday, December 6th, between the hours of 4 and 5 p.m. 3 Jewish youth, approximately from 16 to 18 years, names Bailis, Spielman and Virpownik, were in the process of changing buses. Traveling to their destination, they were confronted by a band of Moslems, who questioned in Russian as to their nationality. They especially asked if they were Jews and immediately proceeded to attack them. I, Szturm Moszko, born 15.12.1920, Poland D.P. #184688, living in Belke Kaserne, came from Goppingen by train at 7 p.m., to the Ulm station.

"I am a heavy metal worker and had gone to Goppingen, the I.R.O. Headquarters to collect my cigarettes. I went out of the station and was on my way to the Gasthaus to have a glass of beer. A tall, dark complexioned man standing near the Gasthaus stopped. He had a mustache and was wearing a raincoat. He asked me in German if I was a Jew. I said "I was," and then he hit me between the eyes with his fist. As he hit me, he said he was an Arab."

—Signed by Szturm Moszko, December 10, 1947

CHAPTER 29

Invasion of Speakers
from Abroad

One year, an assortment of speakers toured our DP camp, fresh from Palestine and America. Speakers who came from Palestine preached Zionism with intentions of recruiting new blood for the newly formed Israeli Armed Forces in preparation for the decisive fight to establish a Jewish State. The cries of the poor parents who got up one morning and found their teenaged children gone, were heard throughout the camp. The young ones escaped and joined the illegal *Aliya,* joining the *Shlikhim,* the people on a mission from Palestine.

Among the speakers were an assortment of celebrated personalities; Yiddish poets, writers, and actors. Even Elea- nor Roosevelt came on a mission both to inquire of the living conditions of the refugees as well as to console the surviving

Eleanor Roosevelt (Center) in DP Camp

remnants. There were also politicians like David Ben-Gurion, first Prime Minister of Israel, who was a splendid orator and impressed the Hindenburg Jewish crowd with his erudition and forcefulness.

Imagine, he addressed the crowd in Yiddish, the language he so abhorred and detested. After the establishment of our Jewish State, he was instrumental in stamping out a two-thousand-year-old Ashkenazi Jewish culture and one thousand years of Yiddish altogether. His plea was to vote "Yes" for the Jewish State when the UN International Commission was about to take a poll among the refugees. The *Shlikhim* (on mission from Palestine), with the purpose of collecting funds and recruiting young people, advised the camp leadership in reeducating the masses toward accepting Hebrew as their mother tongue and Zionism as their political goal.

David Ben Gurion (Center) in DP Camp

The Yiddish language was to be uprooted in our camp, starting with the kindergarten, while the camp population went about their business without paying much attention to the prevailing *Kulturkampf* (*Culture War*). Yiddish was the daily dominant language in all the DP camps, although the Hungarian, Romanian, Russian, and Polish languages were often heard throughout the day. Each one of us children came into the camp speaking different languages, including Polish, Russian, Romanian, and Hungarian; it was the Tower of Babel. Overnight, we all began to communicate in Yiddish, due to the fact that our parents had relaxed and returned to the native vernacular they had spoken at home, no longer fearful of the hostile world. This was the language that united us children, and I soon felt intimate with Yiddish, as my parents had spoken Yiddish to me throughout my life in the Soviet Union, even when I answered them in Russian out of embarrassment in front of my friends.

CHAPTER 30

Hindenburg Kaserne in Action

There was a feud brewing in camp constantly, because the secular Jews used to pester the religious Jews with the inevitable and unanswerable question: "Where was God during our destruction?" When the religious Jews became enraged because they couldn't come up with an acceptable answer, they began writing letters to President Harry S. Truman, complaining that they were being harassed and would he please consider this urgent matter and help them. Somehow this request fell on deaf ears, and Truman never responded.

The religious contingency of our camp kept to themselves. They had their own *shtiblekh* (prayer rooms), a *mikveh* (ritual bath), a kosher kitchen, and a *shoykhet* (ritual slaughterer). Almost all the Jews in camp kept *Shabbes* (the Sabbath), the day of rest.

Every Friday afternoon, my mother would make me carry the *Tcholnt-pot,* the Sabbath meal that cooked for twelve hours on charred oven bricks, to the communal bakery. At midday on *Shabbes,* I used to run with my friends to retrieve the *Tcholnt* and couldn't wait to bite into the brown potatoes and pieces of meat. After *Tcholnt,* we youngsters would sit on the grass, tell stories, and sing songs in Russian, Polish, Yiddish, and Hebrew. I wrote them down in my album.

On a sunny day, the "trade center" was open in Ulm. There were radishes and scallions, beets and apples, among other offerings. Anyone interested in traveling to the town market in Ulm proper

Di fusbalmanszaft.
Ojf dem rechtn fligl der sportlejter Rundsztejn P.

The Soccer Team in Hindenburg-Kaserne (from *Ulm Album*)

could purchase anything available at hand and sell it on our black market. Of the over 900 people in camp, at least 550 of them were employed. The rest occupied themselves with various trades, crafts, black-marketeering, and schemes for how to get rich quickly, not to mention the underworld activities.

My father was the cultural director of the camp. He ran on the Independent ticket and was elected. Most of the board of directors consisted of Zionists of different genres, and they could have easily gotten rid of him, but he was also the unofficial camp police chief, radio announcer, editor of the *Bulletin Board Newspaper,* and had come to be known as the camp intellectual.

In one of his editorials, my father wrote, "We must supply the camp with a piano and turn the huge former German plane installation into a Theater Hall." One morning, Father co-opted a truck and drafted several policemen under his jurisdiction, who took off for some mysterious locale in the city. A few hours later, the crew mysteriously delivered a piano. No one wanted to know how it was obtained.

Kulturamt. Fun links: Niks L., Szmulewicz Ch. un Nadler I.

The Culture Committee, Chaim Schmulewitz (Center) (from *Ulm Album*)

Father organized several strong men, distributed hammers and saws, and supervised the banging and sawing until the German airplane hangar had been converted into a performing arts center. Benches were installed, electric wires drawn, and a makeshift stage built. The theater was used for celebration of weddings and happy occasions. It was also ready for lectures, entertainment, and the screening of Yiddish films.

Once the job was accomplished, Yiddish actors and singers eventually began to flock to our camp. They came from overseas, all the way from America, to bolster the morale and lift the spirits of the survivors. There were writers, speakers, and musicians. Everybody was eager to bring joy to the sad and downcast people.

For the first time in my life I saw Yiddish films, among them *The Dybbuk, Yidl Mitn Fidl,* and *Mamele,* starring Molly Picon and Leon Liebgold, whom I fell head over heels in love with at age eleven.

(Years later, I met Leon Liebgold, during my journalistic days. He was a middle-aged man, bald with a rounded belly, and still entertaining audiences. My childhood dreams were in ruins.)

My father decided that the camp's children must be imbued with a musical education and learn to play the piano. In no time, Father conjured up a master piano tuner who dexterously adjusted the ivory keys, repaired the velvet-covered wooden hammers, and redrew the strings until, to our astonishment, the piano yielded genuinely harmonious tones.

Early in the morning, Moishe, the meal announcer, would clank away at the gigantic frying pan to let the population know that the coffee was ready. "Come and get it, and bring your own coffee pots." As soon as his frying pan rang out the joyous event, the camp population was on the

Der mittog iz fartik!

Moishe, the Meal Announcer. 'Lunch is ready' (from *Ulm Album*)

run. Several times a day, Moishe's frying pan and his "Come and get it" let everybody know that lunch was ready and milk and potatoes were prepared for the children.

Two years had slipped by. Life had since become orderly. Hindenburg Kaserne was alive. As early as seven in the morning, people gathered around the gate—truck drivers, chauffeurs, and auto mechanics—all waiting for transportation into town. Their heated discourse could be heard all over camp. Camp people took politics very seriously. Opinions flew back and forth like arrows. On the agenda was Eretz-Yisrael, (The Land of Israel), Berlin, and camp gossip and its central theme: the Board of Directors.

CHAPTER 31

My Piano Lessons in Camp

Once the piano was repaired and tuned, Father's new brainstorm was to hang up a notice on the camp bulletin board that read: "Enrich your children's lives with a musical education! We will provide the piano teacher."

I was the first child to enlist, and the only one. At the end of the week, Father looked through the registration list and discovered that out of a couple of hundred children, I was the only one who signed up. So he wanted to scrap the entire idea, but felt obliged to hire a music teacher privately, one who would come a few times a week and provide private piano lessons just for me.

Early one morning, a tall, middle-aged, hungry looking German appeared at our doorstep. He bowed courteously to my mother, spoke to her in German, and concluded the terms of his wages. After each lesson, he was to receive a kilo of American noodles. There was no mention of money. The Germans were devastated at that time, having lost the war, their positions, and their former life. He was condescending, and didn't even look at me, as if I was completely irrelevant. I instantly understood that it was a major humiliation for him to sink so low as to teach music to a Jewish child. It appeared, however, that the German's stomach played its own compelling overture in sync with its underfed conductor.

Thus began my musical education. We entered the spacious converted hangar, the furious German and I, his eleven-year-old protégé.

He showed me how to place my fingers on the keyboard and keep time with the metronome he had brought along.

I applied myself diligently to the scales. Each time my fingers slipped in error, the German ground his teeth, slapped both sides of his head and cursed in German, *"Donnerwetter,"* a curse I was already quite familiar with.

I hardly grasped the extent of his hatred; to me, the piano was a symbol of great achievement. I had seen in films how pianists performed famous musical works in front of huge audiences and took their bows to the sound of rapturous applause. I never allowed for the possibility of achieving such stardom myself.

Somewhere on the road, between life and death, children of the war lost the ability to dream. So we lived for the day and gave no heed to the future. Playing the piano became a necessity for me. I found solace in the music, an inkling of a more pleasant world, where one could hope to achieve the yearnings of one's heart. Music reverberated with inspiration, enthusiasm, gentleness, wonder, love, fire, and passion.

The following winter was a harsh one. Snow blocked the roads to the supply area, and the garage-theater-hall where the piano stood was unheated. Though my fingers froze, I wouldn't forego my music lessons, so I put on a pair of warm gloves, cut off the tips of the gloves, and went on playing. The German cursed loudly every time he heard a false note, though he knew full well that the piano hammers were frozen and I had to struggle to get a sound out of them.

In the middle of that particular winter, we suffered a tragic setback. It was bitterly cold in our barracks, including the room that we shared with another family and their two little boys. The room was divided down the middle by an army blanket on a string across two walls, like in the film *It Happened One Night.* We children could barely get out of bed because of the extreme cold. Both fathers decided to go looking for some wood to heat our room.

Our neighbor, Tuvye Schwartz, was a sprightly fellow and he was the first one to climb up to the roof of a deserted garage in our camp, where they found wooden planks on the rooftop. Tuvye took hold of the saw that he had brought along and sliced a wooden plank off the roof.

My father, never very agile, took hold of the saw and plummeted to the ground. An open garage door broke his fall, but injured his ribs and legs. An ambulance was called, and he was taken to the city hospital. People came to tell us the bad news of my father's serious injuries.

You can imagine that, from that moment on, there were frantic trips back and forth to the hospital. Father had broken several ribs, both legs, and both arms. His entire body was enclosed in a cast. At such a time, who could think about music? My mother was consumed with worry, yet we youngsters took it all in stride. So many fathers had disappeared without a trace during the war. I, at least, was confident that my father would recover. Nevertheless, I kept on repeating the few bars of music I had learned in that short period of time, aware that a child of refugees had no right to expect such a luxury, as playing a piano.

DP Police School Certificate

IRO
Commendation
for Chaim
Schmulewitz

THE INTERNATIONAL REFUGEE ORGANIZATION 3.2.49
AREA NO 2 HQS   NELLINGEN   APO 154

1 February 1949

SUBJECT : Commendation.

TO   : Chief of Police - WG 234 Hindenburg Kaserne - Ulm.

THROUGH : Mr. H.S.D.Mac Neal, Field Supervisor
          Sub-Area Ulm.

1. This office has received a report from the Field
Supervisor at Ulm which reveals that had it not been for
your devotion to duty and promptness in the recent incident
involving the individuals concerned in alleged possession
and passing of counterfeit German currency it might well
have been possible that these people may have escaped.

2. The Area Director has much pleasure in commending
and thanking you for your efforts to aid the Occupation Force
and IRO in their efforts to maintain law and order in our
assembly centers.

FOR THE AREA DIRECTOR:

G.E. HARTNELL
Deputy Area Director

CAMP LEADER   Ulm, 4 February 1949
DP Camp WG 234

TO   : Mr. SCHMULEWICZ, Chief of Police, WG 234, Ulm.

I received the above letter from Deputy Area Director, IRO
Area 2, Nellingen. As this letter pertains to you, I, herewith forward
it.

B. Lichtenfeld
Camp
Hindenburg Kaserne

It took five months for my father to recover, whereupon he was sent to Hamburg to attend an "official" police course, returning a week later as a certified police chief with a certificate of achievement. He recruited twenty young policemen in good shape, whose work consisted of guarding the food storage units as well as searching every individual truck that entered through the camp gate, suspecting every visitor of contraband. Their task was also to keep an eye out for the dozens incoming underworld characters.

From the moment my father took over as chief of police, he began to feel concerned not only for the physical safety of the Jews in our camp, but also for their spiritual needs.

CHAPTER 32

THE CASE OF THE STOLEN POLICE FORCE

by Chaim Schmulewitz

THERE ARE FOUR JEWISH DP CAMPS IN OUR TOWN OF ULM, as well as some non-Jewish ones. Here is the story of Ivan Ivanowicz, a resident in one of those non-Jewish camps, who had a wild desire to bring a stolen cow to his point of destination, our camp. Ivan Ivanowicz almost accomplished his task, but with a slight hitch—namely, he was caught by the *Deutsche polizei* (the German police). While under interrogation, he blurted out, "I was delivering this cow to the Jews of Hindenburg Kaserne."

His testimony was like music to the German ears. First of all, a live cow was hard evidence. Secondly, Jewish black marketeers were planning to slaughter a German animal; there was trouble ahead. A party of German police officers, Ivan Ivanowicz, the "innocent victim" and the cow, set out at midnight, straight for Hindenburg Kaserne.

They all stopped close to the gate, put out their lights, and sat in waiting for the Jewish culprits to come through the gate and claim the cow. A Jewish policeman inside the camp noticed a mysterious truck parked on the curb of the road. He promptly reported this account to the sergeant, who in turn also became suspicious, collected his police force, ordered their helmets on, and sticks in hand, they approached the mysterious truck.

Suddenly they were surrounded by the German *polizei* and forced into the truck. In short, the Jewish police force was abducted—helmets, sticks, and all—and disappeared. Only one policeman hid in the bushes, staying behind to alert me, the chief of police. Screaming at the top of his lungs, ready to rouse the whole camp population, I cried out in a voice that could have awakened the dead, "Our entire police force is gone! Someone kidnapped our entire police force!"

Within ten minutes, the entire camp was awake and had congregated in fear. The women wailed, the children whined. Stories were spreading like wildfire of suspicious-looking people roaming the campgrounds. One cannot imagine the nightmare the frightened camp population experienced. Jews in their nightgowns and pajamas. I was the only one who didn't lose his head. I contacted the headquarters of the M.P. (American Military Police), the U.N.N.R.A., and the I.R.O., but to no avail, no one had a clue to what was happening. The camp fell into a *Kol Nidrey* (Day of Atonement) mood.

Towards morning, the police, their helmets, and their nightsticks, showed up. They recounted their story in great detail, to the joy of all camp inhabitants, of this case of mistaken identity, and added that, in the end, Ivan Ivanowicz, the "goy" (gentile), had admitted the whole truth, that he had no Jewish conspirators.

It was *Simkhas Toyre* (joyous Jewish holiday) once again, as everyone kissed and hugged each other and thanked the Lord for being spared.

CHAPTER 33

The Case of
the Stolen Cow

*L*iving at the camp gave the Jews a temporary feeling of security and, above all, a relief from daily obligations and worry. It was a time in limbo, giving the people a chance to recuperate, to sum up their past, to make peace with the present, and to start to contend with the future.

If my memory serves me right, I remember another case with a stolen cow, only this one was actually brought into our camp stealthily. My father, the chief of police, was informed of this piece of news. He immediately set out with several of his policemen in search of the stolen cow. They knocked on every door, searched every living quarter. No cow.

In one of the rooms they searched, there was a man, deathly ill, with his wife sitting at his bedside, putting cold compresses on his forehead and speaking to him in tears. Of course, the Jewish police wouldn't dare interfere; they closed the door behind them and left, but on the way out of the barrack, my father stopped, became suspicious, and ordered all to return to the sickbed.

When they uncovered the patient under the blanket, there was the cow: compresses on its head, its mouth plastered with duct tape. The family was placed under arrest and given over to the ruling German Judicial Court. Their punishment was to be sent on illegal *Aliya* to Palestine.

CHAPTER 34

The Honorary Court of Justice

As an adjunct to a *Beys Din* (rabbinic court), there was established a judicial court of justice in our camp, namely "The Honorary Court of Justice." Three people presided. The court came into session whenever a complaint was lodged. The criminal offenders, which were very rare in camp, were handed over to the German *polizei*. Matters of family disputes were handled by the rabbinic court, known as the Rabbinate. Legal matters were brought before the Honorary Court, none of which were of a serious nature.

One case stands out in particular: Litigations against a Hindenburger inventor of a device that produced counterfeit dollars. This was considered a magic machine. The buyers were convinced that they latched on to a fantastic gadget. When they realized that they had been bamboozled, they came to the Honorary Court to see that justice was served. As the proceedings developed, it became clear that the inventor hadn't forced anyone into buying his device. He claimed that he had never encouraged anyone to break the law. He simply assumed the posture of a real gentleman and considered his invention nothing more than an entertaining device.

The verdict went as follows: The gentleman with the magic machine had to reimburse the plaintiff's money. The gadget was to be disposed of, and if the accused did not adhere to court orders, serious consequences were to follow. Everyone was satisfied.

CHAPTER 35

THE MOST HONORARY
COURT OF JUSTICE

by Chaim Schmulewitz

JEWS! YOU HEAR? MESSIAH'S DAYS ARE NUMBERED, HE'S ON his way, for Moishe Getsl has become a judge over the house of Israel. People finish universities, put in years studying law, invest a wealth of money, and suffer a world of hardship, just to become a lousy jurist. And, here, without as much as knowing the difference between the yeas and nays, I, Moishe Getsl, have become a judge, and not a simple one at that, but rather a Camp Judge.

I can assure you that the Nuremberg Judges can come for legal advice to me, Moishe Getsl, that is, His Honor the Honorary Judge. I run the most democratically effective court in the world. I don't need law, stipulations, or legal doctrines, together with my two assistants, Fayvl Lekish and Pinye Glomp; they are a world of law unto themselves. We are overloaded with work. We satisfy all grieving parties. Both the plaintiffs and the defendants become our best friends right after we are finished with the verdict. Here are some of our cases:

It is well known that both Avrum Gershn and Leyzer Shimshe were born in the same shtetl in Poland. Avrum-Gershn receives packages from the Landsmannschaft (Society of Compatriots) in America, and Leyzer Shimshe does not. So Avrum Gershn is convinced that it is Leyzer Shimshe's doing. Avrum Gershn is accusing his compatriot Leyzer Shimshe of purposely interfering with his receiving care packages from America. Therefore, this particular case is argued before the Honorary Court of Justice with all its Honorary Judges presiding.

Avrum Gershn brought his own witness in the person of Yihide Zaynvl, who belongs to a neighboring Landsmannschaft and is a popular letter writer to the Landsmannschaft in America. He knows for a fact that Leyzer Shimshe didn't write a thing against Avrum Gershn, but Avrum-Gershn is convinced that Leyzer Shimshe did. In this case, it became obvious that Yihide Zaynvl is witness to both the plaintiff and the defendant. To make a long story short, I, Moishe Getsl, the former bookbinder and presiding Honorary Judge, together with my assistants, Fayvl Lekish and Pinye Glomp, a former grocer and a bookkeeper, have come up with the following verdict: "The court is ordering Yihide Zaynvl to write a letter on the spot, one of those tear-jerking letters to the Landsmannschaft in question, and both Moishe Getsl and Leyzer Shimshe are obliged to sign."

It was a pleasure to see former enemies become such good buddies.

Chaim Schmulewitz Court of Justice Article

CHAPTER 36

Cultural and Social Life in Camp

$\mathcal{T}$he refugees in the camps were hungry for cultural expression. This manifested in many ways, including concerts and performances, poetry reading and lectures, but especially in the multitude of Jewish press. A variety of Yiddish newspapers were published in Munich, for and by the refugees, close to a dozen of which followed different political affiliations. These included:

Der Morgn (The Tomorrow) 1949

Dos Yiddishe Vort (The Jewish/Yiddish Word) 1946–1949

Hemshekh (Continuity) 1948–1949

Undzer Veg (Our Way) 1946–1949

Undzer Haynt (Our Today) 1947

Undzer Velt (Our World) 1946–1949

Velt (World) 1947–1948

Yiddishe Bilder (Jewish Scenes) 1947–1948

Yiddisher Invalid (Jewish Invalid) 1947–1948

Yiddishe Shtime (Jewish/Yiddish Voice) 1947–1949

Yiddisher Student (Jewish Student) 1946

Some Yiddish publications were printed in Yiddish but written in Latin letters. Practically every political party had its own newspaper. Almost every DP camp published its own paper. The religious community, including each of its different sects, had its own publications. And, finally, Jewish newspapers were published in Yiddish, Hungarian, Romanian, Polish, Russian, Hebrew, German, and English.

Within a year or two, the cultural directors of the Executive Board in Hindenburg Kaserne hired a teacher who was proficient in the English language, as no one had ever heard English before. The teacher was also engaged in writing letters to the American consulate on behalf of the refugees seeking entry into the United States and other English speaking countries. To us children, hearing English spoken for the first time, it sounded like the speakers had hot potatoes in their mumbling mouths. It sounded like pure gibberish.

In keeping with the expansion of activities in the camp, the Department of Cultural Affairs also supported a soccer team, a sports club, and other sports activities. This was to enhance the health and well being of the refugees. Thankfully, the mortality rate in the DP camps was very low.

Almost immediately, a feeling of kinship developed among the camp residents. They lived and acted as one big family, despite prewar social, economic, and intellectual differences. Having shared the catastrophic experience of war, this community of Jews drew closer together. All previous affiliations with political convictions had been absolved or renewed.

The camp had erased everyone's prewar status and history. For example, before the war, a man of the likes of "Moyshe Bombe" (a nickname), a common porter from Warsaw and an underworld character, couldn't be on friendly terms with the "better" people. But, in camp, he was everybody's favorite policeman. Former prestigious positions and class were wiped away, as they became meaningless and absurd. People who came from a strict Orthodox upbringing became free thinkers, and free thinkers and nonobservant Jews suddenly had an urge for prayer and would don phylacteries and repent.

Orphaned teenagers found warmth and friendship among their neighbors. Families befriended each other and spent many hours together talking, pouring their hearts out to one another, taking daily strolls together, and going to movies and concerts together.

The camp itself consisted of an amalgam of people from all walks of life. Among the nine hundred Jews in our camp, there were rabbis, writers, intellectuals, tailors and shoemakers, cap-makers and carpenters, watchmakers, photographers, doctors, and underworld characters, including former prostitutes whose "careers" had ended due to the abnormal demographic conditions. Among the DP population, there was a surplus of men compared to women. This surplus was mostly apparent in those aged twenty-five to sixty-four. Since women were scarce, they were worth their weight in gold. Every young, middle-aged, or elderly female became a favorable candidate for matrimony, becoming the wives of those men who had lost their families and were now seeking to reestablish a normal existence.

Everything you could find in a well-developed city you found in Hindenburg Kaserne. People socialized in the barber shops and beauty parlors; the bakery; the kosher and non-kosher kitchens, each with its own staff; a meat-supply "magazine"; a canteen run by disabled invalids; a library with Yiddish and Hebrew books; an infirmary with qualified and nonqualified doctors and medical aides; a *gemilas-khesed* (society in charge of charitable aid); a *khevre-kedishe* (burial society); and a *hakhnoses kale* (a fund for poor brides).

Hindenburg gave away in matrimony an orphaned seventeen-year-old girl to a homeless young man from Sedan Kaserne, another camp in town. The residents of Hindenburg threw themselves into this *mitsve* (good deed), heart and soul. The bride was brought by the people before the board of directors with a demand to arrange a Jewish wedding on the camp's premises, with all the trimmings. The board was to provide *nadn* (dowry), *klezmorim* (musicians), a rabbi, and the wedding hall. The people were ready to prepare the wedding feast. The board agreed on one condition: right after the wedding, the couple would immigrate to Palestine to help create the future Jewish State. Everyone agreed, including the couple.

The wedding took place in the big assembly hall in Hindenburg Kaserne. Everyone cooked and baked collectively. A procession of Hindenburger *makhatonim* (future in-laws) escorted the couple to the *khupe* (wedding canopy) with lit candles in hand. The women cried bitter tears remembering the loss of their own children. It was an occasion that brought everyone closer together in agony and joy. As a young child, it made me feel that I was a prominent part of an extended Jewish family.

Jewish DP Camp Hindenburg-Kaserne Ulm/D (from *Ulm Album*)

CHAPTER 37

CAMP SCENES ON THE EVE OF THE PROCLAMATION OF THE NEW STATE OF ISRAEL

by Chaim Schmulewitz

HINDENBURG KASERNE IS TREATED TO DAILY SENSATIONS; otherwise the camp would doze off. Friday, on the eve of the proclamation of the establishment of the new State of Israel, May 14, 1948 (5 Iyar, 5708, according to the Jewish Calendar), the board of directors went into an urgent session. Representatives of all the political parties joined in. Everyone was concerned with one issue: how to celebrate the joyous occasion. Suggestions were exchanged.

What was discovered to everyone's dismay was that Hindenburg has only one single, solitary flagpole that belongs to the Revisionists (political party). More suggestions were exchanged. First things first. A proposal was put forward to borrow the flagpole from the Revisionists and then procure a white and blue flag. Here is where all the trouble began.

As soon as the Revisionists discovered that their flagpole was on the agenda, they immediately split into two groups, the Pro-polesters and the No-polesters. The Pro-polesters declared that it's everyone's celebration, so leave the flagpole alone and let the white and blue flare from the pole of the Revisionists. The No-polesters thundered, "Not on your life! We are not giving up our flagpole. You want to celebrate, go to the forest and get your own flagpole."

The camp director, himself a Revisionist, voted for the use of the pole, causing the entire camp population to split into pros and cons. It took great pains to see the war of nerves calmed down, when the No-polesters threatened that if, by Monday, the flagpole was not in its original place, they will demand extra rations of food.

In no time, the Pro-polesters dug up the Revisionists flagpole, placed it in the center of the camp, and produced a brand new white and blue flag, a feast to behold. As soon as the *Shabbes* (Sabbath) was over, the entire camp population was up and about, getting ready for Sunday's celebration.

Flags were sewn, candles distributed, and cakes were baked. Sunday morning, the camp is scrubbed, cleaned and windows decorated and shiny.

Yesterday, not a flag in sight. On Sunday, five flags were flaring, and to top it all off, the American flag was also unfurled. The gates were decorated with greenery; the Star of David was displayed in every barrack.

Shortly thereafter, the camp police were alerted of a bomb threat. The Jews organized a brigade. Within minutes, the news spread like wild fire that the barracks are mined. Mothers were on the run with their babies; others were searching for their loved ones. That Sunday, after the bomb threats were deemed false, the camp was guarded by the American Military Police as the refugees danced and sang together, cried and laughed while celebrating the most important day in their lives.

CHAPTER 38

Liquidation of the DP Camps

*B*y 1948, the situation of Jews in Germany was deteriorating. Anti-Semitism expressed itself more and more openly. There was only one concern occupying the refugees in the DP camps, namely leaving German soil as soon as possible for their chosen destinations.

The Joint began a wide operation of organizing emigration activities in the American zone of Germany as early as 1946. The Joint was prepared to handle the first rush of applicants. Two years later, news of the partition of Palestine was greeted enthusiastically and raised the hopes and spirits of the people. Possibilities of emigration to other countries soon came into focus.

Visa applications were accepted and proper registration procedures followed: Affidavits were checked; correspondence were carried on with the cooperating oversees agencies or sponsors; medical examinations were arranged for the emigrants; preparations for interviews at consulates were made; passports were put in order; and travel papers, birth certificates, and a variety of other documents had to be obtained or, in cases where proper documentation couldn't be produced, substitutes in the form of sworn testimonies and certified verbal accounts by witnesses had to be presented.

An additional agony and distress befell the refugees, most of whom had no shred of evidence to certify their identities, let alone birth certificates. But this they also overcame. Maybe some of them were con artists who produced false testimonies and documentation, but in order to survive the incredible odds, they had to stay a step ahead of the authorities.

Hindenburg Kaserne was liquidated in 1949. The camp population dispersed. Everyone took the route available to them, and we received a visa and ship passes to America. I, of course, had no idea whatsoever, what America meant or represented, or what to expect.

Years later, wherever Hindenburgers encountered one another, they still felt a kinship. They recalled with warmth and affection those years spent together in Hindenburg Kaserne.

Author's A.E.F. Assembly Center Registration Card
(from International Tracing Service, Bad Arolsen, Germany)

CHAPTER 39

Liquidation
Takes Its Course

*A*s liquidation took its course, most of the Jewish camps were emptied, institutions were closed, buildings were returned to their previous owners, barracks were refilled with incoming refugees or military units, and newspapers printed their closing litany of evidence dealing with the palpitating remnants of survivors who were slowly disappearing, most of them transplanting to the alluvial soil of other lands.

There were around ten thousand survivors who chose to remain permanently in Germany and cast their lot with the future of the West German Republic. The ones who left wanted to leave Germany *Judenrein*—empty of Jews—knowing full well that the Germans were still impregnated with anti-Semitism. But the will of the ten thousand transcended logic. Among them, German Jews, citizens of the Bonn Republic, guaranteed equality and justice under its constitution. Of course, we children were once more unhappy to lose our new friends, the ones we confided in, sang with, danced with, shared personal stories with—the thought that we would never see each other again was a tragic awakening.

Once again, we children were traveling, taking off to unknown shores, changing a way of life, learning a new language and culture, meeting strange people. We were tired, exhausted, to begin anew. Our childish imagination was by now unable to look forward to an unfamiliar way of life. All we lacked was solace, a clean, soft bed, and enough food to still our hunger. Fear was the dominating emotion I felt, as my family prepared for the arduous boat crossing of the Atlantic Ocean.

Author (left) with her Mother (right)

CHAPTER 40

NO MORE DP

by Chaim Schmulewitz

MIRACULOUSLY, I SURVIVED THE HOLOCAUST, WAS PUT into the confines of a refugee camp in Germany, and had bestowed upon me the title of "displaced person." The world went into a frenzy over me. The U.N.N.R.A. was created, followed by the I.R.O. The greatest world powers protected me. World Jewry was overwhelmed by feelings of pity and compassion on my behalf. The Joint experienced the most productive period because of me.

Thousands of officials came to serve me. Jews came from all over the world just to catch a glimpse of me. For three years now the world has been obsessed with me. Some observe me with trepidation, others pity me. Delegations of *shlikhim* (Jews on a mission from Palestine), Parliamentarians, commissions—they all come to observe my psychological state of mind.

I am a theme for writers and politicians. England trembles at my sight. She put at my disposal the entire island of Cyprus. She would give up half of her empire as long as she could keep me away from the shores of Palestine. South America is in awe of me. She closed her borders and refused to let me in, but accepted Hitler's henchmen with open arms. Even if a *mohel* (one who performs circumcisions) or a cantor is needed to serve the Jewish community, Latin America is ready to receive a DP, but not a Jewish one.

Australia is also not at ease. America opened her shores to 205,000 D.P.'s but she didn't mean me.

I became the second front in an extended war. For many, I am an object of subsistence, but not for long. I am on the verge of shedding my label, no more an object of discussion, no more an object of pity or amazement. No more an object of charity. No more a D.P. I am joining the ranks of mankind.

CHAPTER 41

Orientation

*W*hen any camp in Ulm or other cities in Germany were liquidated, the refugees were sent to the Funk Kaserne, located on
the outskirts of Munich. Every displaced person living in the American zone in Germany at that time who had the intention of going to
America had to go through several weeks of orientation before being
given permission to board a military boat at Bremerhäven headed
for the United States.

These were scrutinizing weeks where the displaced persons were
examined physically and mentally and given preparatory Americanization sessions. Of course, children my age were omitted from this
process, but the older ones remember vividly the Americanization
procedure and how it went. Teenagers had to attend the Americanization preparatory sessions, and the American instructor prepared
the refugees for daily discourse in America in this manner:

When you meet an American friend, neighbor, or even relative,
and you are asked, "How are you or how do you do?" remember
that the friend, neighbor, or relative does not want the truth
and is not awaiting to hear your state of mind or the state of
your health, nor something you would want to share with them.
Your reply must always be: "Fine!" or "O.K." and "How are
you?" To this, they will answer, "Fine! Thank you!" And that
should be the extent of the conversation. Americans are not
talkative by nature, let alone interested in your affairs."

Everyone staying in Funk Kaserne put in a day's work and made a slight salary. Women worked in the kitchen; men did menial work.

Everyone was also obliged to be examined by the Central Intelligence Committee, today's CIA. My parents went through an interrogation dealing with their political affiliation. The authorities wanted to know if they were ever committed to Communism. This was during the period of McCarthyism in America. My parents successfully convinced the committee that they were as anti-communist as they could be.

After receiving lung X-rays, my father was informed by the camp doctor that he found a spot on one of his lungs. Of course, Father didn't believe this in the least and began conversing with other people in camp. Eventually, he found out that the doctor was expecting a bribe in order to clear my father for emigration.

Apparently, corruption had its hold even in the transit refugee camps. Father had some pull, and acquired several packs of cigarettes to pay the doctor. He was off the hook and given permission to emigrate.

At one point, we were forced to enter a covered vehicle and were sprayed with some dust. When we asked what it was, we were told that it was DDT, a horrid method of delousing.

We anxiously boarded the SS *General Hersey* at Bremenhoffen, in anticipation of the long and difficult journey across the sea to the Golden Land.

The Author

CHAPTER 42

America the Beautiful

After spending four years in the DP camp as refugees in limbo, we boarded the American military boat called *General Hersey* from Bremerhäven in Germany. I was just a young girl and looking forward to the journey and a new life in America. We were surrounded by a multitude of anxious refugees just like us.

At the start of the journey, I became seriously seasick, but the infirmary was crowded. My mother carried me to the deck so I could catch my breath instead of languishing on the lowest level of the boat. After a while, she became hysterical with worry. Father cornered the ship's doctor, grabbed him by the throat, and warned, "If my child doesn't survive this trip, your life will be in peril." The doctor relented and made room for me in the ship's infirmary where they began pumping intravenous fluid into me. Later I learned that the other patients in the infirmary included the doctor's wife and relatives. Luckily, I recovered.

The minute we left Germany and we passed France's La Manche Canal, we found ourselves in the turbulent waters of the English Channel. The ship tossed and twisted and everybody was afraid. Being in the infirmary for most of the trip, I was not aware of the inevitable difficulties that my shipmates were experiencing.

Two weeks later, our boat finally anchored in Boston Harbor at the end of 1949. To me, the words "Kalamazoo" or "Timbuktu" had the same meaning as the word "Boston." Once on shore, I suddenly felt pangs of hunger. Our entire possessions consisted of two ragged suitcases, the clothes on our backs, and five dollars. Father left my mother to guard the suitcases on land, and we set out along the streets of Boston.

A delectable smell enticed us to the open door of a tavern. There we came across trays of frankfurters, sauerkraut, and mustard. Not knowing one word of English, I pointed to the trays, saying, *"Dus! Dus! Un Dus!"* Apparently, the hot dog vendor knew exactly what I meant, since the sound of the Yiddish words resembled the English equivalent: "This! This! And this!" Father was concerned about having enough money to get to our relatives in New York, so he bought only one hot dog for his hungry little girl. For the first time in my life, I ate a hot dog with mustard and sauerkraut. It was *"Gan Eydn"*—Paradise. I vividly remember those newly discovered, delicious flavors. Father and Mother were elated to know that I had eaten.

From the docks, we were taken by the Jewish agency to the Boston train station, where we boarded the train headed for New York City. We were in such a state of anxiety that we didn't take notice of anything around us. We were led from place to place in a confusing labyrinth of streets, alleyways, crowds, and odors—America.

CHAPTER 43

New York! New York!

ithin several hours, we were at Grand Central Station and looking for a familiar face. Suddenly a blond, middle-aged woman sprang out of the crowd, embracing my mother. It was Frieda Galonska with whom we had spent our years in the DP camp in Germany. She confided to Mother that since she had settled in the Bronx, she came almost daily to the train station to look for a familiar face, thinking, *Who knows?* She might come across a relative. She gave us her telephone number in case we were looking for a place to live. She told Mother that the South Bronx neighborhood where she lived was mostly inhabited by former DP refugees, and that they all helped each other adjust to life in this new land. Later, she helped us find and rent the apartment in the tenement house directly across the street from where she lived.

Still at the station, my father's uncle Didye showed up. My mother and I were totally ignored by the uncle and my father. They joyfully embraced and cried, recalling, in Yiddish, the last time they had seen each other in 1922, when the uncle had the foresight to leave soon to be war-torn Poland for the freedom of America.

We grabbed our belongings and were led to where his car was parked. He had a car. I had never been in an automobile before and imagined that this American uncle must be a millionaire. He drove us to Eastburn Avenue in the Bronx. On the way, we found out that he owned a four-story building, that by profession he was a house painter, and that he was politically to the left of center and his mantra was "Socialism! Down with the capitalists! Fight for the working class!"

Father was baffled by Uncle Didye's politics. Hadn't he heard of Stalin's purges and perfidy? Was he deaf to the suffering of millions of innocent people in the slave labor camps? Didn't America provide him with a great livelihood, security, his own house and food galore? Mother chimed in, reprimanding my father, "Chaim! All in all, you're a half hour in America and already you're talking politics!"

Uncle Didye, a short man with a very pleasant face, rang the doorbell to his apartment. Aunt Mindl opened and the three of us— my father, Chaim, a tall, broad-shouldered man in his early forties; my mother, Tola, petite in size, with curly black hair, in her late thirties; and I, Mirele, sad-faced, drawn, and pale, with Shirley Temple curls—entered into a comfortable-looking place. We were dressed shabbily, carried old suitcases strapped with rope, and really did look like we had just come off the boat.

Aunt Mindl was slightly cross-eyed and in a constant huff. She kept on wiping the tip of her red nose with her soiled apron. One couldn't tell her age. She was a tiny woman, wore a flowery kerchief, and greeted us with a phony little smile.

"Oh! Such welcome guests. Come on in. Put down your suitcases, no one will steal them. Sit down. I will make some food. Later on, I will make you all comfortable on the floor. You see, we don't have room for you people. My dog, Mickey, sleeps on the sofa."

We entered slowly, leaving our suitcases at the door. Uncle Didye was quite hospitable, inviting us to sit down on the plush sofa. He asked me if I was tired after such a long trip. I told him about my ship ordeal and then I asked if English was a very difficult language to learn. We used to say in camp, "All you need to do is pretend you're eating a hot potato. That's English."

He laughed and told us that his wife was no Shakespeare when it came to English. He assured us that, after we ate and rested up awhile, we would see the world around us differently. We were not in Europe anymore.

"Let's see," he said, "how long are you in America now? At least a few hours, while I am here almost thirty years."

Suddenly, Aunt Mindl woke up as if from a stupor. "What do you think, we didn't suffer here from the war, too?" she said. "We had to stand in line for sugar and butter! Can you imagine?"

Uncle Didye couldn't stop her inane chatter; all he could do was shout out, "Shut up, Mindl! You are talking to people that just came back from hell."

Aunt Mindl's words were like spears penetrating my mother's wounded psyche. She was horribly offended; she bit her lip, then lashed out and answered sar-
castically, "Sugar, ha? Butter also? What I would have done during the war, if only I could have stood on such a line with a shortage of sugar and butter!"

Uncle Didye promised my father that, after he rested up that night, he would take him to a job that he had, painting several rooms in an apartment house. He also added that, in my father's profession, it would be tough to get a job, as there was a strong printer's union, the New York Typo-
graphical Union, and they kept newcomers out. So until

The Author with her Parents

he could join the Union, Father needed to do some menial work.

The discussion of the Union led them to a heated argument about socialism and communism and capitalism and the political order of the day. My father had had his fill of his uncle's political ideas, but Uncle Didye urged him to relax. "In the morning, America will look much more enticing. You're in the land of opportunity," he said softly. "It's all up to you. Take advantage of it! Here you can live the American Dream."

Father did not know what Uncle Didye was referring to. Mother was uneasy; she felt lost and disoriented. She worried about what would happen to us and where we would wind up. Tired and sleepy, her eyelids were drooping, and slumber descended upon her face. Suddenly, she perked up, wanting to know where we were going to spend the night.

Aunt Mindl comforted her. "Don't worry, we will cover the carpeted floor in the living room with blankets and pillows, and all three of you will be comfortable for the night."

Sitting on the soiled yellow sofa, all three of us felt comfortable. Here we were, in America, in such a big house, and not a bed to be seen. What a place, this America! All you have to do is put blankets and pillows on the floor. There was no need of beds. But Mother's brain was working overtime. She wanted to rest while Uncle Didye was still chatting away with Father about world politics, the aftermath of the war, the victims, and the victors.

"What about English?" my father inquired.

"Don't worry!" Uncle Didye smiled. "My wife is here over thirty years and still doesn't know the language. When she goes shopping, she counts the streets, and if she makes a wrong turn, the police bring her home."

Aunt Mindl straightened out her kerchief, adjusted her apron, looked at her husband victoriously, and said to us, "Always keep with you the name and address, so that the police can bring you home safely."

"Pay no attention to it, Tola," Uncle Didye said to my mother. "The American police are polite, kind, and helpful, especially to newcomers and the elderly. They know who their customers are."

But Aunt Mindl, fidgety in her discomfort, retorted, "By the time the greenhorns move out, they will leave behind a soiled sofa. Who knows what kind of bugs they brought along with them from the other side?"

I thought Mickey, the dog, resembled a long frankfurter. He wagged his tail constantly and wanted to be patted. As we were lost in thought, Aunt Mindl blurted out, "You know, Didye, we need a new sofa. This one smells! Yesterday, I saw a 'sexual sofa,' not too expensive."

Uncle Didye twitched in anger. "You're forgetting who's the boss in this house, Mindl! The only one who sleeps on the sofa is the dog. When I decide we need a new sofa, we get a new sofa! You just worry about your cooking." He paused. "Besides, it's not a *sexual* sofa, Mindl, it's a *sectional* sofa."

We fell into a deep sleep, convinced that American Jewry awaited

The Author

us with open arms, bated breath, and brotherly love, open to share our tales of woe, horror, and grief. The disappointment came swiftly. Instead, we new immigrants swallowed our tears and went on building anew our shrunken world and the loss of the center of Jewish civilization.

These were our first steps in the Golden Land.

CHAPTER 44

Our First Apartment in America

Within a month, we moved out of Uncle Didye's home and settled in our own place on Cypress Avenue and 136th Street in the South Bronx, in an apartment we found thanks to Frieda Galonska, our neighbor in the DP camp and now our neighbor across the street.

My father found work, not in his chosen profession but in a rag factory, picking out rags of different quality for thirty dollars a week, which was substantial. His uncle helped by lending us three hundred dollars in *shlislgelt* (key money), which the previous tenant of our apartment had demanded under the table. We had to pay it back to the uncle in installments every month. But the place was absolutely magnificent.

We had five rooms, including a kitchen with an icebox, instead of a cold hole in the ground. We had a real oven of our own, hot and cold running water, a bathtub and a toilet, a dining room, a living room, two bedrooms, and a table and chairs the old tenant had left after he moved out. I thought that only a Rothschild could afford to live in such comfort. Even the fairy tales couldn't come up with such a luxurious setting. Mother felt that the apartment was nothing short of a miracle. She said that in Russia, each and every room would have been occupied by a family or two, and there were only three of us, living in five rooms like royalty. Who would believe it? These are the things dreams are made of.

"What do people eat at a big dining room table?" we wondered. We couldn't understand how people could live in so many rooms; we weren't used to such luxury. Mother proposed we all move into one bedroom, and then, slowly, as we got used to living this way, we could attempt to move into the other rooms. So, all three of us moved our luggage into the master bedroom.

We settled like that for a while, until I announced one day, "Mom! I'm moving out!"

"Where are you moving to?" Mother wanted to know.

"Into the empty bedroom. You get me a bed, and I'll have my own room." *Hallelujah!*

Mother soon discovered that when she walked in the streets of our neighborhood, nobody followed her, nobody asked her for papers, and nobody was suspicious of her. "Maybe America has no spies," she thought. "Maybe America is made up exclusively of true and loyal Americans." I was almost thirteen years old, and I was excited at the possibilities that this new world offered. I had my own room, where I cut

The Author

out the photographs of celebrities like Mario Lanza, Gregory Peck, and Elizabeth Taylor and hung them prominently on my wall. I even had my own bed. Several months of bliss passed.

One day, there was a ringing at the door. Mother and I were frightened. *Who can that be? Who is after us?* we wondered.

Mother ran over to the door and asked, *"Ver?"* (Who?)

A man's voice answered loud and clear, "The man who rented you the apartment!"

Mother opened the door inquisitively. Immediately, the old man stepped inside with two suitcases in hand and announced, "I came to stay with you."

Mother and I looked at each other. For a moment we were confused, but we soon regained our composures. The man entered the kitchen, sat down, and made himself comfortable. His forehead was sweaty and his clothes were shabby. Mother didn't know whether to offer him a cup of tea or throw him out.

The man wiped his forehead. He was breathing heavily, and a pathetic look appeared on his face as he began explaining, "You see, lady, my daughter made my life miserable! She threw me out of her house, so I came to stay with you. You have enough rooms."

My mother's cheeks turned red. "Stay with us?" she burst out angrily. "We gave you three hundred dollars that we borrowed from the uncle—money under the table, key money—and that wasn't enough? We are now the new tenants, and we don't need a new tenant, so get your stuff and out you go, before I call the police!"

"Go ahead and call," the man replied, standing. "I am not afraid. You can't even speak English! Nobody will believe you."

At this point, Mother ran outside into the hall and began shouting at the top of her lungs, *"Politsmen! A ganev!* A bandit! A robber! Help! Help!"

Huffing and puffing, the man ran out, and she closed the door behind him.

So this is America, too, we concluded, *full of robbers and thieves.*

That scoundrel didn't know with whom he had started up with. My mother was willing to confront the great dictator Joseph Stalin;

she wasn't going to back down from some insignificant little man in the Bronx.

Father eventually joined the Printer's Union and was sent to work for the New York Yiddish daily called *Di Morgn Freiheit* (Morning Freedom), a left-wing newspaper that ran from 1922 to 1980. Father got used to spending an awful lot of time there, especially when his job consisted of making up headlines that consisted of fake news, distorted truths, and complete Soviet lies. He retired in the 1960s after the Printer's Union shut down and he was left bereft of his pension, in spite of the fact that he had paid thousands of dollars into the Printer's Union in his twenty-five years as a linotyper and printer.

Chaim Schmulewitz at Linotype Machine

CHAPTER 45

Getting Used to America

ownstairs in our apartment building was a little grocery store that was run by a couple that spoke Yiddish, which made it easy for us to communicate our needs. There, we bought every provision, especially the red cans of Chef Boyardee's spaghetti and meatballs and ravioli in tomato sauce. This was a discovery of tremendous benefit. We'd never tasted such delicious cuisine. It was certainly a far cry from my mother's daily chicken soup with *"lokshn"* (noodles) or red borscht and potatoes. Chef Boyardee became my personal chef.

The couple had two American born daughters, both of whom also spoke Yiddish. The older one introduced me to the school she attended, Wilton Junior High School #30, an all-girls public school situated a couple of blocks away. She was a tall girl, well developed, while I was a greenhorn, about five feet tall and in desperate need of a friend.

She and one of our classmates treated me to my first movie in America, *The Wizard of Oz,* which made me so very happy. There was no place like "home." After the movie they took me to an ice cream parlor and ordered a complicated dish called a "banana split." What was a "banana," and why would you split it? I was in seventh heaven; a movie, ice cream, such wonderful American friends, who could have imagined? I appreciated every good turn they bestowed on me.

Wilton Junior High School #30 was the school we attended. To my joy, our daily uniform consisted of a white blouse and a navy skirt, a blessing in disguise, for I had no assortment of clothes to choose from. Nor had my mother ever allowed me to wear a skirt. Ever.

Every morning, we girls were made to say the Pledge of Allegiance and "The Lord's Prayer," a Christian prayer found in the old scriptures of King David's Psalms.

To this day, I still remember the words I chanted then:

Our Father, Thou art in heaven, Halloweth be thy name . . .
. . . thy should be done as on earth as it is in heaven.
—————————

I pledge allegiance to the flag of the United States of America
And to the . . . for which it stands . . .

Of course, I didn't understand a single word of it at the time, but I thought it sounded so beautiful.

The Author's High School Graduation Portrait

Within the first few weeks, my friendship with the grocer's daughter began to crumble. It was on the way home from school one day when my "good" friend turned to me in the middle of the street and announced, "Miriam, we cannot be friends any longer. You do not fit into my group of friends, your English is poor, and they are all American born."

Her revelation struck me like lightning; I was in tears, losing my first friend in America.

After graduation, we lost touch with each other, she was assigned to a good high school, while we refugee girls were sent to what was considered the worst high school in the Bronx, namely, Morris High School, which consisted primarily of blacks, Puerto Ricans, and "greenhorn" refugees like us.

CHAPTER 46

We Found Each Other and the New Dress

𝓘t was in Wilton Junior High School that I met my best friend Feigele. We could communicate in our mother tongue, Yiddish. Our homeroom teacher, Helen Auerbach, taught us American songs like "Daisy, Daisy" and "Let Me Call You Sweetheart."

I still knew no English when, in seventh grade, my class had to take an IQ test. Of course, I and the other Yiddish-speaking students all failed miserably and, in turn, were classified as "retarded" and relegated to a bench in the back of the class. Once this reputation had been acquired, we were expected and destined to achieve nothing.

On the way home from school, Feigele and I would talk, talk, and talk like our hearts were bottomless pits. Never exhausted, we kept on talking all through the day and late into the night. We would take turns accompanying one another home, and this went on for several years.

What was it that we talked about? Search me! The same goes for Feigele; she also has no clue about what occupied our minds at that particular time. It must have been our unhappy homes or our lack of money, though in my case we had a little money so we never felt poor. I was also an only child and my father worked in a Union shop, whereas Feigele's stepfather, who never worked a day in his life, was supported by his American brother who had come to the States before the war and settled in the South. As time passed, Feigele and I talked about shoes and dresses, hats and purses, necklaces and earrings—that's what the two of us craved. I imagine we also talked about boys. During the summers, we sometimes worked together in the nearby 5&10 Store, selling little items and earning fifty cents an hour.

When I approached Mother for a new dress, and she heard that it would cost seven dollars, you'd think the sky was about to fall. For her, shelling out that kind of money for a dress was reason enough to have a fit.

"What's the matter?" Mother would demand with a grimace on her face. "You don't have enough *shmates* (rags)? Look in your closet and you'll find a whole department store! You think your father is a Rothschild or a Rockefeller? When I was your age, I wore hand-me-downs for all occasions, and we were stuck in the Great Depression. Not like you! You're stuck in the lap of luxury."

Feigele and I were reaching our teenage years, when girls are interested in boys and boys in girls. I shed copious tears and pestered my mother, insisting that all the girls owned new dresses and I was the only one dressed in discarded rags. No boy would ask me out for a date, let alone dance with me. I would wind up an old maid, and it would be all her doing.

With Feigele, the outcome was altogether different. She had the stepfather who was unsuited for any kind of employment, and in addition there were two hungry, runny-nosed toddlers and an old grandfather to care for. How could she be so heartless as to ask for money for a dress?

But dance we must. Isn't it obvious? Naturally! So I devised a clever scheme: We were both miniature five-footers, weighing barely ninety pounds each, so I agreed to share my new wardrobe with Feigele. Somehow I managed to wangle out of my mother seven dollars for a blue flowery dress with a fitted waist and no sleeves. It fit me as though I had been poured into it. I wound up having two dresses, while Feigele had none.

I deliberated with myself and decided Feigele would be the first one to wear my new blue dress, and I would wear the old dress in which I was as comfortable as a fish in water. The question at stake was how to manage it without my mother's knowledge. We wracked our brains and furrowed our brows until we conjured up a solu-tion. I would put my new blue dress into a brown paper bag and throw it out the window. Feigele would catch it, go back to the staircase of my house, take off her old dress under the stairs of my building and stuff it into our mailbox, and put on my new dress. To our joy, it fit her like a glove, too.

The Author (right) with Feigele

That evening, our plan was carried out to perfection. Feigele, looking like a princess, dressed in my new blue dress, and I, in my old worn-out dress, was still as pretty as a doll. Off we went to the Diplomat Hotel in Manhattan.

When we reached the hall at the Diplomat, it was already jump-ing with young people, most of them the offspring of Holocaust survivors. Youthful couples paired off. The eyes of the older girls popped out, hoping to attract and snag a bridegroom. Feigele and I, still teenagers, were bent only on having a good time and dancing the night away. And although all the young boys and girls had been in America just a couple of years and had never before had occasion to dance, we mastered the waltzes and tangoes, the cha-chas and sambas with great aplomb. As always, Feigele and I were a popular item; a bunch of young fellows attached themselves to us and treated us to Coca Colas and pretzels.

A photographer appeared on the scene and snapped our pic-tures in a variety of poses. Almost at dawn, we blissfully allowed the fellows to escort us home to the Bronx. Not only had everything proceeded without a hitch, but Feigele was pleased with her cavalier, my old DP camp friend Muniele, the guy who eventually became her intended. After the dance, she reversed the process, and the blue dress wound up hanging innocently in my closet as if it had been there all evening long.

The Author (2nd from right) with Feigele and Muniele

Then, chapter two of the saga! The photos from the fantastic dance eventually arrived. Mother and I gazed at them. Feigele and I were two beauties! Truthfully, you could sell tickets for a peek at our images. The two handsome young men stood alongside us, smiling. My mother was ecstatic until suddenly, a blood-curdling scream pierced the air in our kitchen. Everything turned black before my eyes; Mother had caught on.

She finally found her speaking voice and addressed me with cutting irony. "Tell me, Mirele, the dress Feigele is wearing looks to me exactly like your new blue dress. What is it doing on Feigele?"

I began to stutter. "Yes! No. You are imagining things! Don't try to confuse me!"

My mother was adamant, shrieking like one possessed. Her features were distorted with contempt toward me, her only child. "I know already your tricks, Mirl! For what does your father slave day and night? So that your friends should have new clothes to go partying? Remember, you'll pay for this lie. Hell will freeze over before you weasel any more money out of me for anything again."

Today, "Feigele" lives on 5th Avenue, and owns a wardrobe designed exclusively for her.

Half a century has gone by, during which we have worn out thousands of dresses and danced at hundreds of affairs, but the taste of that long-gone evening lingers, ever fixed in our memories with the warning: "Don't forget where you come from!"

The Author (left) with Feigele

CHAPTER 47

My First Romance

While I attended the worst high school in the Bronx, on the weekends, I was spellbound by the works of Leo Tolstoy's *Anna Karenina*, Gustav Flaubert's *Madame Bovary*, Emil Zola's *Nana*, and Alexander Dumas's *Camille*. I read and reread all of these novels in my all-Yiddish literature course, given by the master Professor Kharlash at the Jewish Teacher's Seminary in Manhattan. As I read these novels, I felt the inner pangs of their tragic romances, lived symbiotically through the heroines, and above all, I was in love with love.

In the early 1950s, my good friend Muniele, who was now engaged to Feigele, called to tell me that he was now a soldier, stationed in Fort Meade, a military base, just a short train ride from New York. He had met another soldier who spoke a fluent Yiddish, and wanted to introduce us. "You have to meet him," he concluded joyously. "You'll fit like a glove!"

I was now seventeen and the soldier was twenty-three. I was still a greenhorn; he was an American. I was diminutive in stature; he was a six-footer, a college boy, with a mane of curly black locks. He even drove a car.

The first time we met was at our home, under my mother's watchful eye, and he immediately became my mother's *liebling* (darling). He knew how to gain her confidence with his servile attitude toward her. "Dear Mrs. Schmulewitz!" he would say. "You're such a good cook!" As a matter of fact, my mother was a terrible cook.

Moyshe used to come to my house on weekends from the military base, all sweaty from the summer heat, and he would ask if he could take a shower. My mother thought it was a sign of courting, though I wasn't aware of such masculine displays of intimacy.

Moyshe

We were considered a couple. All my girlfriends were envious of such a great catch. A college boy, an American, a fluent Yiddish speaker—how I had managed to trap such a whale of a guy was all a mystery to them.

As time passed, he wanted to impress me, relating to me that his father was a famous Yiddish poet. Even with my having read an extensive amount of Yiddish poetry, I never came across his father's writings. To tell the truth, I wasn't used to Moyshe's love declarations, due to the fact they didn't stop in this car, in nightclubs, while dancing—it was a constant "Love you! Love you! Love you!" I couldn't imagine that love could be so annoying.

In time, Moyshe began describing our future life together, the little house on Long Island where we would live, the three children we would have, preferably two boys and one girl. Here is where I drew the line: "How do you know that I'll be able to have any children?" I demanded to know. "After all, I am so petite and weigh a measly ninety pounds!"

He smiled. "Only frigid women are barren and cannot conceive."

Of course, at that time I didn't knew what "frigid" meant, but I figured it must be related to a Frigidaire.

"We will live in a little house on Long Island," Moyshe continued wistfully, "and when I return from work every evening, the dinner will be ready on the table, the fireplace will be crackling with gusto, my slippers ready for the leisurely life, and we and our three children will sit around the fireplace, with marshmallows on a stick, and we'll sing Yiddish songs. One big, happy family. . . ."

I don't know where I found the nerve or the inner strength to conjure up my opposition. "My dear Moyshe!" I cut in, contradicting his declaration of love and our happy, stable future together. "I think you are missing an important facet of our future life together! How odd, but you never asked me about my dream! After all, it involves both of us."

But, of course, Moyshe was con-fident that young girls, recent new-comers from a disastrous world, could have no dreams. He was obsessed with his design of life, and at the same time, he was convinced that he was making a young greenhorn girl happy, handing her the American Dream on a silver platter.

The Author

Time didn't stand still, and the Korean War was raging. Moyshe informed me that they were sending him to Okinawa, and I began to feel the tragedy of our impending separation. At that moment, I sensed that there was no love without tragedy. War scenes awoke war-torn childhood memories in me, and I suddenly felt the tragedy of love and life, just like the characters in those novels I had read. We all felt the pangs of sorrow.

Upon hearing this news, a friend suddenly turned to me with a question. "I heard that Moyshe is being sent off to Okinawa. Did he at least bestow upon you a diamond engagement ring, as a token of his love? And, if for any reason he didn't, there is only one solution, and that is to do what all the other girls are doing."

I realized she was referring to the conjugal bed. "You know I'm a decent girl, and an honorable one to boot," I replied emphatically. "No monkey business as far as I'm concerned."

Moyshe and I spent our last evening together in a nightclub. I confided in him my girlfriend's advice about the conjugal bed. He had no compunction and had nothing against it. Little did he know how enraged I would be by his attitude.

"Moyshe! Don't you know by now that I am a decent and honorable girl and not like the other girls? If I would do a thing like that, I would have to go up to the top of the Empire State Building and throw myself down all the one hundred and eight floors!"

He was insulted. "Is that what I am worth to you?" he wanted to know.

He took me home to the Bronx in his car, and we promised to write. The problem was that he was no Romeo, while I was an authentic Juliet. I could write lyrical letters, full of expressions of love, while he kept on sending me photos of himself from Okinawa, surrounded by geisha girls around a swimming pool, with his arms outstretched as if to say, "But I love only you!"

Once again, time was on the run, and the Korean War came to an end. Moyshe called me from Seattle, Washington, where his plane had landed. I was to know he came home in one piece. Aside from "Love you! Love you!" he told me he'd be flying into Idlewild Airport (which is today's John F. Kennedy International Airport) and that his parents and relatives would greet him and take him home to Long Island.

I was devastated that he didn't even invite me to greet him at the airport. After all the love letters, all the "love yous." Although I had hardly heard of Idlewild Airport, didn't even know where it was situated, and had no money for a taxi, all that occupied my mind was, "I should have been there to greet him."

I spent a sleepless night, hurt, resentful, filled with anguish, and thinking, *Where did all these love declarations go?*

Next day, the phone rang. It was Moyshe. "Love you! Love you! Love you!" He informed me that he couldn't wait to see me and within the hour he'd be at my house.

"Moyshe!" I said, exasperated. "Put the brakes on! We're not meeting in my house! What I will do is meet you halfway, on 14th Street in Manhattan. I've worked out a plan of action for us."

We met across the street from Klein's Department Store on 14th Street in Manhattan. He was ready to pounce, to grab me for joy, but I interrupted this outburst. "Listen to me, Moyshe!" I made it slow and precise, "I have come up with a plan. Let us stop seeing each other for the next three months. You date other girls, I'll date other fellows. After three months, if our love will endure this separation and we will still be in love as before you left for Okinawa, then we will know that we are made for each other."

He agreed, and the instant he agreed, I knew that Moyshe was not for me. Real love doesn't take furloughs, nor does it take a three-month respite.

Three months passed, and I dated young men, curious to find out my own worth. I was capable of attracting educated, intelligent, and scholarly young men—guys to my liking—and lo and behold, there they were, as nice as they come!

After three months, the phone

The Author

rang and rang off the hook, and I sensed it was Moyshe as I picked up the receiver. He told me that he had gone out with all sorts of girls, but none of them had come up to his expectations. He also informed me that he had acquired the keys to our mutual friend's apartment in Manhattan, and only there would he be able to explain to me in detail how he felt about me after these three months.

I knew precisely what he meant by "acquiring the keys" to an apartment, thinking to myself, *It will probably wind up with the conjugal bed after all. Here I dealt with a soldier who just returned from the war zone. . . . He will once again surround me with his 'Love! Love! Love!' and kisses, and I will once again feel the distinct rift of the two worlds that separate us.*

With one exception, I was prepared for this event. Before I left home, I decided to take along my good friend Bashke to keep me from falling into a trap. I advised her to pinch me when she saw I was relenting.

Bashke was one of ten siblings, all new immigrants like us, only a few years in America. They stemmed from a hick little village somewhere in the outskirts of Warsaw. Neither Bashke nor her siblings were ever schooled, except for the youngest who still held on to his mother's apron. Bashke's English and Yiddish vocabulary was quite limited, she never read, and she could hardly write. Boys shied away from her due to her slow mental capacity. I kept her as a friend because she was good-hearted, soft-spoken, and wanted to study.

When Moyshe opened the door of the apartment, he realized that I was not alone, and he looked at me with great scorn in his eyes as if to say, "You tricked me! What a nasty thing to do!"

We entered the living room of the apartment, which was neatly kept, and sat down on the sofa, while he closed the door behind him, got on his knees, and began a new approach.

"Let's elope this minute!" he murmured. "I'm ready!"

I stared at him in disbelief. "Listen to me, Moyshe!" I exclaimed, "My mother loves you, you would make her very happy, but I have nothing to hide. If I ever marry, I would like to do it in a big, illuminated hall, full of invited guests, dressed in a beautiful bridal gown. Besides, no one stands in my way, so why should I elope?"

Moyshe was dumbstruck; the look in his eyes revealed anger and humiliation, loss of face and regret. He was embarrassed in front of my friend Bashke. Instead of winning the hand of a submissive and subservient little girl, he had been outright rejected by a self-assured, confident immigrant girl and, on top of it, in front of her friend.

"Come on, I'll take you home!" was all he could say.

That afternoon, he took me home first, where we said our good-byes very politely, wishing each other a good life, and then he took Bashke to her home a few blocks away, parked his car in front of her stoop, and proposed to her. Bashke agreed to marry him on the spot. After all he was an American, a college boy, fluent in Yiddish, and would provide a good living.

And wonder of wonders, they eloped, settled in the little house on Long Island, had three children, two girls and a boy, and sat in front of the fireplace together often. His slippers were ready when he came home from work, the dinner was already on the table, and above all, she was submissive and subservient. They were a couple made in Heaven. *Bashert*—meant to be.

How do I know all this? First of all, we remained good friends. And second, several years later, my husband and I visited them in Long Island where I had the opportunity to see firsthand how my life would have turned out had I accepted Moyshe's proposal.

The Author (right)
with Bashke

CHAPTER 48

Mother's in Distress (At the Dentist's and Loretta Young)

ne sunny afternoon [in 1953], we had a very pleasant visitor, Frieda Galonska, our neighbor from across the street.

She and my mother settled on the sofa in the living room to watch Liberace on television. Liberace played on a gilded baby grand piano, a lit chandelier glimmering overhead, his mother's photograph adorning the piano, and his older brother playing the violin nearby. Both women envied the mother of these two talented musicians for having such well-turned-out sons.

"Did you ever see such a beautiful smile on a man's face?" my mother blurted out.

The two shook their heads in collusion. Only in America. Then Frieda let out a long sigh, indicating that was about to spill the beans on her son, Larry, who was by then twenty years old and in danger of being drafted. She complained bitterly that he didn't want to get a job because he had to learn English first.

"He can go to night school, they learn them English there," my mother insisted.

Frieda took a hanky out of her pocket and began shedding tears. "He also insists that everybody else his age is called up to the army, and I say to him, 'Bite your tongue. This is why I came to America?

To lose my only child in Korea, after what we went through?' But the kids today don't listen, you know. He insists if he's called up, he'll join the army and go."

Suddenly, my mother was grateful for having a daughter and not a son.

Frieda had come up with an idea of how to keep him from joining the army. She had suggested he go to the dentist, pull out all his teeth, and put in dentures. She'd heard the army didn't accept young men who wore dentures. "But he got angry at me," she said.

Mother cringed. "Why should he pull out all his teeth when he is already nursing a bald spot?" she asked Frieda. "How is he going to get married? The American girls of today are very picky! They want teeth and they want hair, they want a car and a guy with a job and money in the bank and furniture . . ."

After Liberace, *I Love Lucy* came on, which both my mother and Frieda loved. Absorbed in the show, both women forgot for a moment about the war, laughing and sighing at the same time. I watched with them, and got upset when they kept trying to foretell what the outcome of the show was going to be.

My mother's favorite was *The Loretta Young Show*. Loretta's beauty dazzled my mother, as did her gracious appearance onto the screen, her majestic entrance into the television studio, and her magnificent dress unfurling. All along, Loretta smiled, displaying her beautiful mouth of the whitest and most perfectly set teeth. They were like pearls.

Mother opened her mouth, showing her compatriot her missing front tooth.

"How about going to a dentist?" Frieda suggested.

On the other hand, who ever heard of going to a dentist in our time? Mother's teeth had always been in ship-shape condition, so there was no need to start bothering them now. But Frieda, who was an expert on teeth since her Larry had refused to get dentures, said that if one tooth falls out, the rest of them have a tendency to follow. "Tola," she said, "nearby, on Brook Avenue, lives an American dentist. Pay him a visit."

My mother decided to take Frieda's advice and paid a visit to Dr. Feldman. The dentist wanted to know how long Mother had been in America, and how she liked America, and wasn't it a wonderful country? My mother agreed, adding, "If you don't have trouble with your teeth!"

Dr. Feldman wanted to know if she brushed her teeth every day and what toothpaste she used. Mother told him, "It depends. Where I comes from, nobody brushed their teeth, just the rich people probably did. Who could afford such a luxury?"

The dentist suggested she sit in a special chair and open her mouth wide so he could take a look at what was going on with her teeth. At the end, he concluded that she was missing a front tooth.

"That's why I'm here!" she said triumphantly, "I don't want to look unattractive, I want to look American."

The dentist smiled and asked her if she watched *The Loretta Young Show.*

"Who doesn't?" she replied. "Isn't she the most gorgeous actress?"

The dentist smiled fiendishly. "You must have noticed her perfect teeth."

Mother agreed. "They are beautiful."

Dr. Feldman didn't let up. "I want you to know that Loretta Young wears dentures and that's what makes her so beautiful, so I am going to suggest, instead of putting in just one tooth, why not take out all of them and put in dentures, like Loretta Young? I will make you beautiful, you'll have perfect dentures, and nobody will know. Everybody does it today; it's in style! Every woman wants to look young and beautiful, so once I finish with your mouth, you will also look young and beautiful, like Loretta Young."

My mother leaned back in the dentist's chair, thinking she was in the prime of her life, so why not compete with Loretta Young? After all, she was in America, the land of opportunity. For a moment, she saw herself floating into the house on Cypress Avenue and 136th Street in the Bronx as if she had just come out of a television set. All she has to do was buy the kind of dress Loretta wore and put in dentures! The dentist was not about to disturb her daydreams; he knew that dealing with greenhorns could be quite profitable.

"So what do you say? If you are ready, so am I. You'll be the toast of the town with your new dentures, you'll see."

Mother agreed. "Go ahead," she said, "just make me beautiful."

Getting home that afternoon without a tooth in her mouth, she was greeted with a surprised look on my face, which changed colors with every breath I took.

"Ma! I think you went too far with your Americanization, and why do you want to look like Loretta Young for? Don't you know it's the makeup, the lighting, the dresses, and they do it to sell a product?"

My pleas didn't touch her; she insisted on one thing: "I want to be beautiful like Loretta Young. Wait till I get my dentures. I will be a new woman on the block. No more the old Tola, I will be the new Tola!"

The Author's Parents

As soon as the new dentures were installed, Mother felt they were like roller-skates, prancing about within the contours of her mouth. She couldn't understand how Loretta Young's dentures were so perfect and hers were such a mess. As soon as my father arrived home from work, he took one look at her and broke out in a screaming huff.

"What did you need dentures for?" he railed. "The dentist took you for a ride. An American swindler! He cheated you out of my hard-earned money! Now take him to the Pripetchik Supreme Court. The literal translation of the Yiddish word Pripetchik is a "fireplace," but this idiomatic reference is to an imaginary fictional town with a fictional Supreme Court, "

The mood in the house became toxic. But my mother stood her ground. "He promised to make me look like Loretta Young!" she cried.

"Who is Loretta Young?" Father wanted to know.

"She is a film star, the most beautiful actress on television, who also wears dentures."

Father's blood was curdling. He wanted to know if the same dentist made the dentures for Loretta Young, too. The dentures were knocking against Mother's gums, and he was at his wits end. He didn't let up; his anger grew by the minute.

"The dentures that the actress wore were probably done in Hollywood, by another dentist," he said. "You should have gone to her dentist."

"What's the matter?" my mother persisted, whimpering. "You don't want a beautiful wife?"

Father roared. But there was no use talking; she kept on insisting she had done it for him. By this time, he was in a state of revulsion, and she clutched her head in both hands, whining. "The problem with you men," she snapped, "is that you don't need nothing! All you need is your food on the table, and whether it's me or a gorilla without teeth, you wouldn't know the difference. There was a time when boys used to tell me that I was beautiful."

"What boys?" he shouted.

"I won't tell you or you'll be jealous."

Father was visibly at his wit's end. "I couldn't care less! Where are my glasses, my pills, and where did you hide my newspaper?"

At this point, Mother felt lost and insulted; all she could think of was the dentures that were floating around in her mouth like two gondolas in Venice. She knew that she had been carried away for a moment by America's promises. Father didn't console her, but instead insisted on knowing where his glasses and paper were hidden.

"In the Frigidaire! Where else?" she shouted. "Men! When will you fix your heads so that we women could live in peace?"

Father was getting tired of the combat, so he ended it with disdain. "I don't care what you look like, by me, consider yourself beautiful."

Author's Article "My Mother and Loretta Young" (Published in the *Forward*)

The Author

CHAPTER 49

My Husband, Mendl

Among the first volunteers to arrive in Europe after the war were American Jewish scholars. They organized young men and began collecting scholarly and valuable secular and sacred books. Included were entire Jewish libraries and art objects that had been looted and plundered in Eastern, Western, and Central Europe by the Nazis, headed by Hitler's Rozenberg-Shtab, whose aim it was to erect a Museum of the dead Jewish people in Frankfurt after Hitler's victory.

Among the Americans who were packing these books into boxes was Professor Kopl Pinson of Queens College, with his young assistant whose name was Mendl Hoffman (later to be my husband).

Mendl Hoffman was ten years my senior and had studied Jewish history at Columbia University with the world-famous historian Professor Salo Baron. Mendl stemmed from a little town in the Carpathian Mountains that had three levels, Upper Apshe, Middle Apshe, and Lower Apshe. Later, the family settled in Bereksas, a village nearby. His father, Avrum, was a *Vizhnitzeh Khasid*, belonging to the Vizhnitz

Mendl Hoffman

Sect of Hassidim. He was also a *Melamed,* a teacher of scripture for young boys.

Early on, as the war was progressing, the Hungarian municipality made an effort to get rid of its entire Jewish population by declaring all Jewish families illegitimate. The reason given: the parents in such families were not married in a church, therefore the children were declared illegitimate bastards. So even though their father's name was Itzkowitz, Mendl and his siblings had to take on their mother's maiden name, which was Moskowitz.

Furthermore, Mendl's mother's marriage was declared illegitimate, so they had to take on her mother's maiden name, which was Miller. The grandmother's marriage was declared illegitimate; they became Tabac. And so it went down the family line until they reached the name Hoffman.

There were seven of them, three boys and four girls. In 1944, Eichmann and his Nazi Hungarian cohorts, called *Niloshes,* invaded the Carpathian Mountains. The villages where the Jews had been living peacefully for generations were surrounded and evacuated into a ghetto, until finally the Jews were herded into cattle cars and transported to the Auschwitz-Birkenau death camp.

Mendl's older brother Yosl succeeded in escaping, and he joined Tito's resistance army in Yugoslavia. Mendl, a fourteen-year-old at the time, worked during the war years in a bakery in Budapest. Worried about the welfare of his parents and siblings, he decided to go home to Bereksas, with a loaf of bread in his back pocket.

When he arrived, he found himself caught up in the evacuation of the Jewish population of the village. They were being lined up to be taken first to a ghetto and eventually to the death camp. Among them were Mendl's twelve-year-old brother, Benyumin; his mother, Bluma, and his father, Avrum Chaim, in their late thirties; and two of his older sisters, Nekha and Rayze. Upon arrival in Auschwitz, they were immediately confronted by the selection. All were sent to the left by order of the infamous Dr. Mengele. Mendl

The Hoffman siblings in the shtetl Apshitze (in the Carpathian Mountains)

was young and strong and wound up on the right. A young fellow standing next to Mendl pushed him slightly and said, "Look up the chimney, kid. There go your father, mother, and all your siblings up in smoke."

Of course, Mendl had no clue about what was happening around him. While digging ditches, he got sick and was sent to the infirmary. There he wound up on an upper level cot, while underneath him lay the bedridden son of a famous rabbi, whose Hassidim revealed to the outside kapos that the famous rabbi's son was in need of help. Everyone complied; they brought him medicine, food, and water, and the young man was recuperating.

Meanwhile, a group of Yiddish actors, fresh from the Lodz ghetto, who were prisoners in the camp, were brought into the infirmary to entertain the Rabbi's son. The actors appeared baffled and incoherent, but instantaneously began performing Sholem Aleichem's satiric sketch, *"Kasrilevke Brent"* (Kasrilevke is Burning).

Suddenly Mendl woke up. Never in his life had he ever heard of Yiddish Theater, of Yiddish actors, nor of Sholem Aleichem, the most famous of Yiddish writers. He had also never heard of secular Jews. Mendl couldn't stop laughing, looking at the bizarre scene. The rabbi's son underneath Mendl's cot looked up and enjoyed the young kid's laughter to such an extent that, from then on, he shared with him his medicine, food, and drink. It's quite possible that due to this Yiddish troupe of actors, Mendl recuperated enough to join the death march to Austria.

It was a bitter winter at the end of 1944, with freezing winds twisting all around them. The victims had neither winter clothes nor boots to protect them from frostbite. Many of them died on the march, but Mendl survived to reach another concentration camp called Ebensee, situated in a picturesque Austrian village surrounded by three beautiful lakes. Gravely ill, he was thrown onto a pile of corpses and left for dead.

Mendl (Mikolasz) Hoffman

Soon he heard a commotion, and with his last ounce of strength, he clawed his way out of the pile of corpses and saw that the gates of the concentration camp were wide open. The cowardly Nazi guards had run away, and the suddenly free inmates were running around seeking revenge on those who had made them suffer, namely the kapos, the inmates who were chosen by the Nazis to brutally keep order in the camp. One of the inmates had a sharp knife, which he swiftly plunged into a kapo's chest. Ripping open his jacket, the inmates discovered a loaf of bread hidden inside. Everyone devoured the blood-drenched bread, and so did Mendl, who then walked out of the gates, wandered through the streets of the town, and collapsed in front of a private little house.

When he awoke, he found two elderly Austrian sisters taking care of him. They washed him and fed him, realizing full well that he was a Jewish boy, one of the death camp's victims. Knowing that the war was over, the Germans and the Austrians were frightened at the thought of the many survivors seeking revenge.

Mendl, weighing only sixty pounds, recovered and left for his village, looking for any family members who might have survived. He discovered that his brother Yosl had pulled through, as had his two sisters, Esther, twenty, and Sara, seventeen.

To everybody's surprise, only a single village girl named Eby returned, having survived in the Wallenberg Houses in Budapest. She came back with her father and brother. The minute Yosl laid eyes on her, he was smitten. Nothing mattered any longer, not his surviving sisters or his teenage brother. He asked Eby to marry him, but the girl refused on the grounds that she had had a boyfriend before the war and was hoping that he had also survived. She approached the love-stricken Yosl with a proposition: "Tell your little brother, Mendl, to go to Budapest to search for my boyfriend," she said firmly and without any concern for his feelings. "If he finds him, I will not marry you, but if he doesn't find him, then I will agree to be your wife."

To begin with, Yosl was in his late twenties, almost bald, and not to Eby's liking. But love conquers all. To please his brother, Mendl took the train to Budapest, found the boyfriend, who was already married to someone else, and came back home with the good news. Eby, devastated that her love had married another, immediately consented to marry Yosl. The groom was under a trance, leaving his siblings to fend for themselves, forgetting that, as the eldest brother, it was his responsibility and duty to care for them after such a catastrophe. Seeing that there was no one to depend on, both sisters decided to leave for illegal *Aliya* to Palestine.

Meanwhile, Mendl left for Germany and settled in a DP camp where he met up with Professor Kopl Pinson of Queens College. Dr. Pinson was on assignment to gather all the looted Jewish books, pack them into boxes, and send them off to the YIVO Institute for

Jewish Research in New York and to the University of Jerusalem Library.

During the war, the Nazis attempted to plunder the European continent of all Jewish cultural artifacts. Hitler himself assigned his *Rosenberg Shtab* to build a Museum for a Dead People in the city of Frankfurt. The work of gathering these looted books was beyond Dr. Pinson's ability to handle on his

Mendl (left) with Dr. Kopel Pinson (2nd from right)

own, so he recruited nineteen-year-old Mendl to help him out. After several months, Dr. Pinson realized that Mendl was a very bright young man, so he decided to send him off to America to his sister and her husband, Dr. and Mrs. Siff, who at that time lived in the Bronx. In 1946, Mendl boarded the second boat of orphans headed for America and was met by his newly adopted family.

The dwelling of the Siff's was always full of guests, mostly intellectuals, among them Alexander Fyodorovich Kerensky (1881–1970), former Prime Minister of Russia, who never returned to his homeland and died in America, in the Bronx. Mrs. Siff accompanied Mendl to Taft High School, and when he studied at City College, she made him sandwiches every day.

In 1953, out of deep appreciation for America, Mendl enlisted in the U.S. Army and was sent overseas. There he learned the computer skills that came in very handy later in his career. By the time we got to know each other, when Mendl sat in on my courses at the Jewish Teacher's Seminary, he was already twenty-nine and I was only nineteen. The year was 1955.

I was an avid reader of Russian, French, and German literature, all in Yiddish. I happened to read a novel entitled *Nokh Alemen* (*The*

Mendl in the Armed Services (1st row, 1st on right)

End of It All) by Dovid Bergelson for a Yiddish literature course at the Seminary right around the time I met Mendl. The hero of the book was named Mendl, and his love interest was named Mirele, like me. The boy in the novel came from a small village somewhere in the Carpathian Mountains, just like Mendl, and he was very bright, very sweet, and very much in love. He was blond with gray eyes and high cheekbones, and was very down to earth. On top of all that, he was quite brilliant.

At first, after meeting Mendl, I was reluctant; he did not fit my sense of tall, dark, and handsome. But he was very gentle and good. He began pursuing me by coming to the Jewish Teacher's Seminary, sitting in on my literature classes, and taking me home by subway.

He offered to take me to Chekhov's play *The Cherry Orchard* in Greenwich Village. And from that first date on, we saw each other every single day for almost a year, talking without a stop, until he said, "We are getting married in June, aren't we?"

To which I replied, "Definitely not!"

He turned pale. "What do you mean by not?"

"I mean to say, Mendl, that we are not getting married in June," I replied. "We are getting married in September."

Father admired Mendl; he found in him a brilliant young man. Mother was very unhappy. She protested, "What's the matter, you have no time? Look around, there are plenty of fish in the fish store."

I corrected her. "In the sea, Mom."

"There, too," she replied. "Look around you!" She wanted to convince me. "You might find a good catch, a boy with a car, with money in the bank, a good family—what's the hurry?"

As usual, I disregarded her pleas. "I'm not interested, Mom. I don't need a car, I don't need money. I need a boy I love."

"Love, shmov! What do you know about love? Look around! Maybe you can get a better bargain."

"What's a good bargain, Ma?"

She didn't let up. "You have no taste in men. By me, a good catch is a tall, dark, and handsome boy, a man with black eyes and curly black hair . . . but what's the hurry? You

Mendl Graduating City College

can hardly wipe your nose properly, and already you run under the canopy."

"Ma!" I replied. "I'm not asking your permission. We're in America now, and besides, we're getting married next year."

"That is America talking! Parents don't count here! What's the big deal with him? So he can read a book and he can count!

I can also read a book and count at the same time, so someone is snatching me?"

My father was happy, but when he sat down to eat his dinner, she piped up, "This time, Chaim, you better eat fast, your daughter is getting married!" He paid very little attention to her.

I am still full of gratitude to the seminary, where I attended evenings through 1957. There I received a multicultural education that included world history, world and Yiddish literature, Hebrew, psychology, sociology, and the entire spectrum of a rounded curriculum. All the courses were given in Yiddish by Yiddish-speaking scholars and educators. Luckily, the Seminary conducted a literary contest at the end of every semester. The chosen topic of my essay was, "What Constitutes My Judaism?"

I won the First Prize—A $350 Literary Award, in 1956, the same year I became a bride.

The Author graduates from Jewish Teacher's Seminary
(1st row, 1st on right)

What attracted me to Mendl? I swore I would never marry a Holocaust survivor because I knew what that entailed, not only psychologically. He was ten years my senior, balding, with one lazy eye, and he had no money. None. He had ten dirty pairs of socks and five dirty shirts to his name. He worked for Professor Lodge at Teachers College, Columbia University, helping the doctoral students at Watson's Laboratory work on statistical tests and measurements on the earliest computer.

And I fell in love with him. He was brilliant and gentle and constituted my kind of Judaism.

What would I do with such an enormous amount of prize money?

Mendl

CHAPTER 50

"THE WEDDING DRESS"

Yiddish Forward, 1955

*(Translated from the Yiddish by the author
and Beverly Koenigsberg)*

SEVERAL TIMES DURING THESE PAST FEW DAYS I'VE BEEN thinking about my wedding dress. Don't ask me why. Lots of memories unaccountably rattle around in a person's head; who can fathom the machinery of the human brain? But let me proceed with my story. It took place more than fifty years ago when I was still a youngster, a *"tsutsik,"* as my mother referred to me. I worked all day and in the evenings attended the Jewish Teacher's Seminary. For three years, I toughed it out on the subways, traveling from the Bronx to Manhattan and back. After working at his job, my father would wait for me at the train station, fearful of letting me walk home on my own late at night in the South Bronx.

Mendl would pick me up at home before every date. My father liked him very much. My mother was far from pleased with the match.

"What's your big rush?" she badgered. "You are only half-baked, you can't even properly wipe your nose, and you want to plunge into marriage? And whom have you picked? Your taste is nothing like mine! You know I would like someone young, tall, broad-shouldered and masculine, with a full head of curly black hair, a man who turns you into jelly when he looks at you. Like Moishe. Instead, you picked a crossed-eyed old *'Bock'* (Buck) with thinning hair, and not a penny to his name. Where are your eyes, Mirl?"

My mother nagged me incessantly. "You have just turned nineteen and he's ten years older than you. Wonderful possibilities for husbands are bumbling around out there, but you are in a mad rush. What's the emergency? *Oy!* I am so miserable."

My mother carried on in this manner night and day, but to absolutely no avail. Mother hadn't anticipated that her compliant little girl would suddenly have the guts to defy her.

"Modern children," she moaned, in chorus with parents of her own generation. "No respect for their elders."

And so, the months flew by until it was high time to look for a wedding dress. On this subject, my mother took on a new life. She forgot that the match was not to her liking, because at last she would have the opportunity to fulfill one of the principal functions of motherhood. It was no piddling matter; she was going to buy a wedding dress for her little girl. She herself had been attached without marriage to my father in a slave labor camp in Siberia. She certainly had no wedding either. Now, at last, she had the opportunity to choose a dress that would express her individual preference.

My mother took me to Orchard Street on the Lower East Side to hunt for bargain wedding dresses. We didn't have much money in those days, so she began by appraising the ready-made, extra-large, way-out-of-style wedding gowns. And since I was miniature in size weighing about ninety pounds, including my ribbons and huge clumps of Shirley Temple curls, you could hardly find me inside those large creations. Every time a saleswoman struggled to get me into an outsized wedding dress, she would grab the dress by the shoulders, lift it up and say: You see, it's going to fit perfectly." She looked at my mother and implored, "It doesn't matter how wide or long it is. That can all be adjusted. The important thing is that YOU should like it."

I turned up my nose at all these dresses, imagining how I would climb down the steps and no one would see me inside the dress, and my poor groom would have to search under the wide sleeves to uncover my little hand for the wedding ring, for without my hand he couldn't lead me to the bridal canopy. I would be lost in one of those wedding gown monstrosities.

When I arose from my reverie, I observed the saleslady confidently clutching a wedding gown and assuring my mother, "When we finish altering this dress, she will look like a doll, a regular doll."

Mother started to bargain. " Sixty dollars . . . Fifty dollars . . . "

I sat on the side, buried deep in thought. *Once in a lifetime a girl gets married. Why not be the most beautiful bride?* Yet, there I was, faced with a major catastrophe. I'd rather not get married at all than consent to be an ugly bride. I jumped out of my chair and announced to Mother, "Mom! Stop bargaining, I wouldn't get a wedding dress here if they gave it to me for nothing! Forget it. I might not get married at all!"

My mother, glaring at me with a vicious streak in her eyes, poured out her embittered heart. "What do you think, my fancy daughter, that you are Rothschild's pet horse? Your father works like a dog all day, and you are too good for Orchard Street? Since when have you become accustomed to anything better?"

I postponed buying a wedding dress for quite a while and settled down to await a miracle. At the time, I worked in a Millinery Concern opposite Lord and Taylor's, a costly and exclusive department store on Fifth Avenue. I stared in awe at the manikins in the window, fitted out in the beautiful bridal gowns a young woman might only imagine. Of course, I thought to myself, in those bridal gowns any girl could be a "Beauty Queen." But those were only idle dreams. I would never have dared even to cross the threshold of such a hallowed establishment.

But the Jewish Teachers Seminary announced the $350 literary contest first prize. This was a formidable sum in 1956, one that my father would have had to work a full month to earn. I rolled up my sleeves and sat up nights writing feverishly and fast. I fell asleep at the table and could barely get up in the morning to go to work. I was falling off my feet, erasing, correcting, rewriting. Time was up, and with a twinge in my heart, I submitted the essay.

The days and weeks stretched on. There was no news. As it was the end of the school year, preparations were underway for the graduation, teacher's diplomas, and the distribution of prizes. I ran around like a chicken without a head, thinking, *What should I expect? What's in store for me?*

With a broad smile, my beloved literature teacher, Chaim Kazhdan, with his thick white hair, genial mustache, and his amiability and love for us students shining through from his mild eyes, prepared to announce the names of the prizewinners. Knowing full well that his students were prepared to leap through flames for him, he took his papers out of his brief case, shuffling through them back and forth a few times. Finally he laughed heartily and announced,

The Author and her Parents

"The first prize in the literary contest was won by Miriam Schmulewitz!"

Everyone applauded. I remained in my seat, speechless, unable to utter even one single word, while before my eyes I could see it—my wedding dress.

I will be a beautiful bride after all.

When the moment arrived for me to accept that astonishing check from the Esther and Louis Segal Foundation, I could barely catch my breath. I was supposed to say a few words of gratitude to the judges, but all I can recall was whispering to my teacher that I am about to pass out. He reached into his pocket, extracted an aspirin, and handed it to me with a half glass of water.

I managed to survive that evening. My mother, Father, and my groom, Mendl, all glowed with pride.

Quite early the next morning, I took the check out from my drawer and went directly to the store of the magnates, Lord and Taylor's, on Fifth Avenue, just as though I were the child of a Rothschild. I rode the escalator to the upper floor, collapsed into a plush couch, and asked to be shown catalogues of bridal gowns.

The Author with Mendl

At first, the elegant salesladies looked me over with a smirk on their lips, for not only did I look nothing like a Rothschild's daughter, I wouldn't even pass for one of Rockefeller's upstairs handmaidens. But I assured the salesladies that they could rely on me and displayed before them my vast fortune.

They put me on a literal pedestal while I showed them the most beautiful and elegant wedding dress from the pages of those catalogues, ignoring the fact that the model was tall, slim, and fit as a fiddle. I wanted to know only one thing: "Will I look as pretty as the model?" And this they guaranteed without a shred of doubt. They measured me and weighed me and dressed me up in a corset, like Scarlet O'Hara in *Gone with the Wind,* a pair of high-heeled white shoes, and a veil strewn with pearls, and just like magic, overnight, I became a $350 princess.

Mother lamented the $350. "How in the world could you have been so heartless and spent a fortune on a wedding dress that you wear only once in a lifetime? Only a robber could have done such a thing! Not to mention keeping it a secret from your mother. You could have had a complete living room and bedroom set for that money. You didn't even ask for my advice!"

Her weeping went on and on, but it was a *fait accompli*. I had won that day. I was the most beautiful bride the world had ever seen.

The Author in
The Wedding Dress

CHAPTER 51

Mother's Last Act

The wedding took place in Burnside Manor in the Bronx, and the elite of the Yiddish world were invited, including great historians, writers, linguists, and academicians—all Mendl's friends. The orchestra was led by the renowned composer and musician Lazar Weiner.

Once the wedding was over, Mendl and I remained standing in the middle of the hall with Mendl's brother Yosl, his wife Eby and my father and mother. Mother was still clutching her pocketbook close to her heart, completely in a daze, unaware of what had just taken place. She turned to me, and said, "Okay, Mirele! You ate enough?"

"Yes, Mom!" I replied. "I ate enough."

"Did you dance enough?"

"Yes, Mom, I danced enough."

"Did you have a good time?"

"Yes, Mom, I had a good time."

"In that case, come on home."

I was stunned. "But Mom," I insisted, "I just got married! I'm not coming home with you. I'm going home with him, with Mendl, my new husband."

Mother was still confused. "Doesn't he have an apartment?" she wanted to know.

"Yes, Mom! Now it's our apartment!"

Mother ended up a very morose, dejected and melancholy person, living like so many others, in Miami Beach. It seems she missed those years in Russia when she was heroic, stood up to Stalin himself, and saved us from a deadly end. In America, she lost her interest in life altogether, except for dancing every Friday on Collins Ave and 72nd Street. She also went to night school, but instead of studying English, she took up the philosopher Spinoza as her way of showing off that she was different.

Otherwise, she stayed home, falling asleep in front of the blaring television. When Mother died in 1988, the four of us—my husband, Mendl, my two sons, Avrum (Avi) and Benyumin (Ben), and myself—all came from New York to the funeral. Practically none of her friends showed up. But the last scene at her funeral is stuck in my mind forever. It was my father who turned to me with his last request.

"Do me a favor, Mirele," he pleaded with me, "I would like to see your mother for the last time. Can they bring her out so I can say good-bye to her?"

"Surely, Father," I assured him. "I will ask the mortician to do this for you."

So we went down to the morgue, and they brought out Mother's body. Father bent over and kissed her fro-

The Author's Parents

zen lips, exclaiming, "Oy Tola, Tola, all these years you refused to turn on the air conditioner, and now you're in the freezer!"

On the way to the gravesite, Father requested one thing: "When I die, bury me with an umbrella so I can poke her in the ribs."

CHAPTER 52

A Pure Miracle

The love of music has stayed with me since my early days in the DP camp.

In the 1980s, I wrote my first musical play called *Reflections of a Lost Poet,* based on the life and works of the most beloved Yiddish bard, Itzik Manger.

At that time, I was doing my graduate studies at Columbia University when I met a classmate named Rena Borow. I asked her whether she was interested in collaborating with me on a musical play I was in the midst of writing. Without any hesitation, she obliged, and we began writing together. The result was a hit Off-Broadway musical called *Lieder fun Gan Eydn* (Songs of Paradise).

In the midst of the writing, Rena asked me, "Who are we writing it for?"

I replied, "For the drawer! But I do have a premonition that this play will have a future."

In 1982, I had a weekly column in the Yiddish newspaper *The Forverts* (Forward). Among the many celebrities I interviewed was the world-famous impresario and founder of the New York Shakespeare Festival and the Public Theater, Joseph Papp, whose Jewish name was Yosele Papirovsky. I stumbled upon him innocently, not really familiar with his accomplishments and fame. I was in the right place at the right time .

The Author with Joseph Papp

Joe Papp had rediscovered his Jewish roots and the Yiddish language he had spoken at home in Brooklyn as a child. We hit it off splendidly. He loved to speak Yiddish with me and asked me to translate Shakespeare into Yiddish. I complied. Joe became attached to my family and me. He was involved with the YIVO Institute for Jewish Research, the most renowned Yiddish scholarly institution in the world. He produced yearly benefits for YIVO with the help of famous Broadway and Hollywood stars. One of them always had to sing a Broadway popular song in Yiddish, which I had translated.

At one of the rehearsals, among many stars were Tony Randall and Jack Klugman. Joe came in on the holiday of Purim with a shopping bag, took out a little gift wrapped in gold paper, and handed it to Tony Randall. Tony unwrapped it to reveal a Chanukah dreydl, a special spinning top. Everyone began to laugh—after all, it was the holiday of Purim, not Chanukah. Tony took out a card that read:

Roses are reddish,
Violets are blueish,
If not for Christmas—
We'd all be Jewish!

To everyone's delight, Tony Randall and Jack Klugman sat down on the floor and began playing dreydl.

Joe Papp was the one who produced *Songs of Paradise,* in Yiddish with English interpolation, at the Public Theater in New York. It played for almost a year—eight performances a week to sold-out houses and great press reviews, especially in *The New York Times.* On January 24, 1989, Richard Shepard wrote, "There is surely nothing now on stage in New York that is more sprightly, in any of our city's many tongues, than *Songs of Paradise,* the first production of the Joseph Papp Yiddish Theater."

Since then, I have written many plays and many articles, but the most exciting times were the years I spent with Joseph Papp.

The Author with Theo Bikel and Fyvush Finkel

The Author (center) with Jerry Stiller and Anne Meara
(Mendl and son Avi on left)

The Author with Leonard Nimoy

CHAPTER 53

Yatzek

In the 1980s, I flew to Poland with the cast of one of my plays. On the way back home to America, with LOT Airlines, we all made ourselves comfortable in our seats. Sitting near me was a young Polish man who didn't stop staring at me. I ignored him and directed my gaze in a different direction. But he refused to let up; he smiled saccharine-sweetly, but the expression on his ruddy, close-shaven face was strained. An hour or two elapsed, and I decided to put an end to the silence. I turned toward him and asked him in English, "What's going on?"

He was delighted, rested his third glass of vodka and orange juice on the tray, stirred it with a swizzle stick for a second or two and finally engaged me in a conversation also in English. "You're Jewish, aren't you?"

I threw a little smile his way. "What makes you think so?"

He invited me to sit next to him, and proceeded with great satisfaction. "I am Yatzek," he said. "You understand," he said as he slowly sipped his drink, "I have a proven method which detects Jews from a distance. There is an anthropological study, which I apply to total strangers, and it works like a clock. Not even once have I failed to identify a Jew."

"And why are you so impetuously curious to identify Jews?" I wanted to know.

"Whatever do you mean?" He licked the moisture from his lips. "It has become an obsession with me, whenever I spot a person, I want to know immediately if I'm right, and the method I employ is fool-proof."

"Well, then," I retorted, "let's hear how skillful you are in recognizing a Jew."

The Polish young man was roused, as though he were about to reveal a secret that had been hidden behind locked doors. "Here is how it goes," he said, lowering his voice as if in confidence. "A reliable anthropological study has shown that if you draw a fine line from the undermost tip of your earlobe to the tip of your nose, and the line is parallel to the floor, it is a sign that the face is that of a Jew. This cannot be denied. It's common knowledge, even to my Jewish friends."

"How frightfully interesting." I assumed a joking tone of voice. "I am actually not familiar with that particular study, though I am familiar with another anthropological study that falls into the category that all Poles are fools!"

The young man didn't even blink an eye. He ordered another vodka, smiled broadly, and replied, "Yes! It's true, I agree with that anthropological study. I, too, believe that all Poles are idiots; it's a well-known fact that cannot be denied."

I peered into his large, laughing eyes, replying, "I have never actually seen such an anthropological study with my own eyes, exactly as you, Yatzek, have never laid eyes on this improvised anthropological study from which you quote. For that reason, I want to tell you that Hitler didn't request any anthropological studies from the Jews, the Poles, the Gypsies, the gays, the sick, the old, the young, the brilliant or the fools. When he wanted to get hold of a Jew, he devised his own anthropological study, and we both know the outcome of it all."

"Hitler! He had very bad advisers."

"But nevertheless, he still met with success in eliminating a third of our people with talk such as that."

Yatzek was slowly beginning to understand that he had slipped into a knotty spot, and it was going to involve a struggle for him to untangle himself.

"You understand, Yatzek," I continued to take him to task, "Polish anti-Semitism is an old and difficult illness. You swallow it with your mother's milk. With you, *The Protocols of the Elders of Zion* is a holy text. Every Sunday in church, you get your portion of the sermon dealing with Jewish hatred from the priest, who pounds into you the old refrain that we Jews killed your god, who, by the way, was also Jewish. That is why it is important for you to recognize a Jew, to search for signs—a long nose, black hair, from the earlobe to the tip of the nose draws a straight line parallel to the floor. And what about a Jew who loses his nose? How will you be able to recognize him, Yatzek? How good it is to hate, Yatzek? How easy? It blends so readily with the mood of the vodka that you swallow every few minutes!

"You have just told me that you are on your way to work in America. You will work in a casino, a luxury liner, in roofing. You won't be home for almost an entire year. Whom will you love along the way? A stranger? Whom does your wife love when you're not around back home? It's a tough way to make a living, Yatzek. Did somebody screw you so that you cannot stay in Krakow and earn your bit of bread like everyone else? You want to conquer the world, and who is preventing you from accomplishing this? The ones with the straight lines stretched from their earlobes to the tips of their noses? You look for a way to stay in America, and who is to blame because it doesn't work out? The ones with the straight lines to their noses, because they occupy all the government positions, own all the real estate in Manhattan? All the banks? The World Media?

"But consider it, Yatzek, after living in America for five years, you can become an American citizen and boast with great pride, 'I am an American!' But we Jews, after a millennia of Jewish life in Poland, never were treated as equal citizens. And do you know why, Yatzek?

Because the Poles kept reminding us that we were living in Poland as boarders and that they were our hosts. In contrast, you want to absorb all of America in five years. And do you know why? Because America welcomes immigrants with open arms, no matter what religion, race, or creed, and gives them equal rights. But when Poland was invaded, Yatzek, during the Second World War, most of them gave up their Jews, with rare exceptions. Poland was an accomplice to our fate. No wonder Hitler chose Poland to build his crematories and gas chambers! And you, Yatzek, who can barely speak English, want in just a few years what your people would not bestow upon their rightful citizens, the Jews, in a course of a thousand years!"

All at once, Yatzek stopped ordering drinks and straightened up in his seat, his blubbery blue eyes suddenly watered over with a gray mist. He clutched my hand and began kissing it and shouting. "I am a cockroach!" he cried out as if possessed. "You can trample me with your boots, step on me as if I were a worm, because I deserve it! I promise you that such words will never again pass my lips. I will stop seeking out Jews and measuring the length of their ears and noses. I understand. I understand what you are saying; only I never heard such things before. You can imagine that they never taught us these things in school. When I graduated from Krakow Professional School, I was one of the guides for groups of Jewish visitors to Auschwitz. I cannot forgive myself! No one ever spoke so openly to me before. Forgive me! If you would like, smash me like a cockroach, it would give me relief."

When the plane landed, Yatzek followed behind me like a puppy, carried my bags, held doors open for me, and we parted like good old friends. As we exited into the cold air at Kennedy airport, he still kept shouting, "Don't worry. There won't ever be anymore . . ." And from a distance, he drew the line from the earlobe to the nose, laughing, "Nevermore!"[1]

---

1. A version of the foregoing story originally appeared in the *Yiddish Forward* and was translated from Yiddish by the author and Beverly Koenigsberg.

This reminds me of a female Polish guide in Auschwitz, who emphasized that Jews and Poles were both exterminated and burned in the gas chambers. When the white smoke poured out of the chimney, these were the ashes of the Poles. When the black smoke appeared, these were the ashes of the Jews.

I shall end this chapter with an incident that occurred to my good friend Lillian, who finished our Hebrew School in Ulm, Germany, two years before I did, and upon the suggestion of a friend, decided to enroll in a German Gymnasium in Munich in 1948. Her professor in this German high school refused to explain to her an algebraic equation she did not understand, with these words: "Under different circumstances, you would have been ash in my ashtray." Lillian confronted the principal, whose response was, "What am I to do? I have to hire whoever was available, and most of the skilled teachers were gone."

The Author with her family (from left: Mendl, son Ben, Chaim, Miriam, son Avi)

CHAPTER 54

Further Reflections—
Deciphering Historical Moments

$\mathcal{W}$e are a people who are "a breed apart" from the rest of the so-called "civilized" world. Who could have accomplished within a four- to five-year period in the DP transit camps, the miracle of renewal we achieved? Unlike other refugee-status people in the world, past or present, we have endured in times of adversity and retained our stamina, our tenacity, our courage, and our determination in the face of enormous loss and suffering.

It seems that the world needs an outlet for its constant bestial brutality. Our shield and triumph against the savage world after the Holocaust—after what we went through, millennia after millennia, as scapegoats at the mercy of the nations of the world—was our tenacity to survive as a people.

My assumption leads me to believe that we began building our national homeland not only in Palestine, but in every DP camp throughout Germany, France, and Italy. Every one of our DP transit camps could have been considered a miniature Jewish state. With the rebirth of our left, right, and center

The Author

174

political parties in the camps, we resuscitated our cultural life, religious affiliations, schooling, and art, as well as restoring our belief in humanity—*not* a small feat.

We began to solidify a version of our "homeland" along the way to redemption. The refugees of all ages, the young, stateless Jews, consolidated, created, and joined those who went to Palestine prepared to fight, to sacrifice their own lives *Al Kidush Hashem* (in the name of God), as well as renewing the age-old solemn oath never to forget Jerusalem.

~

We are also a people with a history of building, rebuilding, and destroying our own historical and cultural heritage. To illustrate, I will mention my husband, Mendl, my son Avi, and our youngest son, Benyumin, who was born in Israel in 1970, a year after we settled there.

Once we moved into our own home on Israeli soil, in a village called Herzlia Pituakh on the outskirts of the town of Herzlia, next to the Mediterranean Sea, a neighbor came by to greet us with a bouquet of multicolored

The Author with Mendl

flowers. She greeted us with a hefty, *"Bruchim Habayim!* Welcome your coming to Israel," adding, "Now you can stop being a Jew and start being an Israeli."

Of course, I was stunned and bewildered and just blurted, "We came to settle in Israel precisely because we are Jews and not Israelis!"

And that ended our association.

We spoke Yiddish in the house, and I spoke to my children three languages concurrently, Yiddish, Hebrew, and English, and it worked out well.

Mendl's family, as well as the people on the street, the kindergarten, and the neighbors all made fun of my little boys, who spoke fluent Yiddish. They began to pester me that my children would be outcasts, the laughingstocks of all they came in contact with.

While both my children spoke fluent English with their English-speaking friends, outside the home, they spoke Hebrew, but at home we spoke Yiddish. The family didn't give up; they resented the Yiddish they had spoken all their lives They tried to prove to me that Yiddish was not a language, that it had no grammar, that it was a hodgepodge of German and other infiltrator languages.

That's when I decided to take up Arabic, get myself a tutor, and *"Shukran Allah!"* (Thanks to God!), I had a new weapon to argue my case. I called together Mendl's family and presented them with a lecture of what Hebrew is fused with, how many Middle Eastern languages make up its linguistic combination. I think I accomplished my task well; they never mentioned the subject again.

In 1973, we lived through the Yom Kippur War in Israel. I was left alone in the house with my three-year-old, Israeli-born Benyumin and my father, who was with me throughout this ordeal. My eldest son, Avi, an actor born in the Bronx, and my husband, Mendl, who had now become a theatrical producer, were working in the theater together, and they set out to entertain the troops on the front lines.

Mendl drove the truck with all the actors, sets, and costumes to the Golan Heights in the middle of the battles that were raging. I, on the other hand, questioned the whole situation. I was hysterical. The news kept coming back that the attacking Arab forces were decapitating Israeli soldiers and publicly displaying their severed heads.

A thought hit me: *What are we doing here in Israel? Another war, with my loved ones at the front?* After all, my husband had survived Auschwitz and lost his entire family within several minutes. . . .

I waxed nostalgic for the boring commercials on American television and missed them desperately, just to be able to relax for a while. Surrounded by dire danger and treacherous enemies, I understood that Israel was a political entity, and that war was necessary to defend and protect the Jewish state, but I wished that we could return to America, where it was safe. A few years later, my family and I did move back to the United States.

The Jewish historian Shimon Dubnow (1860–1941) believed that the "survival kit" of the Jewish people consisted of our faith, our culture, and our being dispersed throughout the four corners of the world. That way, if one Jewish community was wiped out—God forbid—other Jewish settlements survived. This arrangement had worked for two thousand years.

Since our move back to the United States, I have dedicated my life and career to the preservation of the Yiddish language and Jewish culture.

Throughout history, there has never been a people that has banned the use of its own language. But through a century of assimilation and neglect, the rich Yiddish language and culture was abandoned by the very powers that should have celebrated it. After the Holocaust, a new and proud Jew was about to be re-created and reinvented, not only in America but in the new State of Israel.

No more Holocaust! Hooray! No more guilty feelings! Bravo! No more Yiddish. "How could we have gone like sheep to the slaughter"?

The answer to this absurd accusation was brilliantly expressed in the poem by the greatest Yiddish writer and poet Chaim Grade:

Desolate Prayer Houses

Translated by Miriam Hoffman from the Yiddish

Why didn't we resist? You want to know?
You saved your own skin—
While you demand of us, the ones who perished,
To have also saved your conceited dignity and honor—
So you could brag to the outside world,
That you are the last of the exterminated heroes.

We, who carried our young on our shoulders,
Our wives and the old folks,
We, who were tortured—
To the point of losing our image of God—
We, who were stripped naked,
Of us you demand chivalry?
We, with our dead hands—
Should have upheld your dignity
Among the nations of the world—
Who prostrate before power
But not before those who suffer?
And what about your pals from afar—
As well as the free world?
What have they done?
Did they get down on all fours—
Pleading for our rescue?

Why didn't you surround and protect us—
The mighty and powerful of the world?
Why didn't you line the streets
With your bodies—
To prevent our massacre?

Why didn't you starve yourself to death?
Why didn't you tear your garments for our dead?
Every single day,
Every single hour,
And every single moment?
Where was your Jewish devotion to us?
And of us you demand Esau's might?
He who says that we are responsible
For our weakness—
Has no compassion in his heart!

Shmil Duvid and
Bluma Itzkovich
(Hoffman) (Mendl's
grandparents)

Our history does not start with the Holocaust, nor does it begin with the establishment of the Jewish State. It starts with our EVOLUTION as a people, with our own considerable authentic culture. Today we are on the periphery of forgetfulness and the obliteration of our own cultural and historic past. At stake is our Jewish heritage, both in Israel and in America, should we abandon the memory and history of our past.

Thus, I draw upon this wealth of our scholarship, its wisdom and wit, its tragic events as well as its triumphant moments in our history. It is said that the soul of a people rests within its language, and language is culture.

The Hebrew alphabet has its own etymology but other than modern-day Israel, it lacks a geographic home base. Yiddish is not the official language of any specific country. Yiddish is a fusion language, just like other languages of the world. It's considered an Ashkenazi-European language fused with German, Aramaic, Latin, Greek, and Slavic, as well as Hebrew, which is a Semitic vernacular fused with Canaanite, Sumerian, Egyptian, Persian, Aramaic, Arabic, Greek, and Latin.

The Hebrew alphabet, just like all of the Semitic languages, is written from right to left for the simple reason that written communication in the pre-biblical era in the Middle East started with pictorials known as cuneiforms that demanded chiseling on stone from right to left, a writing system that began in ancient Mesopotamia in 2600 B.C.

George Orwell once said, "He who controls the past, controls the future," to which I would add, "He who doesn't control his past loses his future!"

Yiddish kept our religion alive for generations, together with *Loshn-Koydesh* (the sacred tongue of biblical Hebrew/Aramaic), while Aramaic is used exclusively in the prayer houses and prayer books. Plus, Aramaic is also used only in official documents like the *Ksube* (the Ketubah, the Jewish marriage license), the Haggadah, which is read on the holiday of Passover, and the *Kaddish* (the prayer for the dead).

With the creation of the Jewish State of Israel, Yiddish theater was banned, Yiddish press rejected, Yiddish schools denied, and TV and radio allowed for one hour of Yiddish programming on occasion and that only after significant protests. The rejection of Yiddish reminds me of the decrees to which the English Empire subjected her satellites, rejecting Welsh, Irish, and Scottish and forcing upon them the Queen's English. But, as of late, the British have come to their senses and restored their colonial languages to their proper domiciles. I am confident that this will also happen with Yiddish, in spite of the long neglect, and the passing of the Holocaust generation.

The new Jew has undergone a lobotomy or maybe a glioblastoma—in other words, brain surgery—to eliminate the memory of two thousand years of exile, including its greatest cultural accomplishments, creativity, and historical facts.

By not restoring the wealth of our cultural accomplishments, American Jews began assimilating at great speed, depriving their future generations of their linguistic heritage. The exceptions to the rule were the Yeshivah academies that flourished after the Holocaust. This resulted from their all-consuming fear of losing their hold on Orthodoxy, not to mention the ultra-Orthodox who created a great national divide between Orthodoxy and the enclaves of secular Jewry world over. It is also high time to mention that the Orthodoxy committed a grave injustice by removing themselves completely from the Jewish secular world, depriving their curriculum of the great accomplishments of both pious and secular Jews who contributed a vast amount of literary prowess in the fields of rabbinic literature, cultural, historical and literary content, as well as our input into the fields of science, biology, chemistry and medicine.

Such lost knowledge can be found in the works of Maimonides, known also as Rambam or Rabbi Moses ben Maimon (1135–1204), who was a most renowned Medieval Jewish philosopher, scholar, and thinker. He wrote commentary on the Mishnah, a basic part of the Talmud compiled around 200 A.D. by Rabbi Judah ha-Nasi. Rambam's 13 Articles of Faith are predominant in Jewish law.

Barukh Spinoza (1623–1677), a Dutch philosopher of great renown, was of Portuguese-Jewish origin. His perceived heretical beliefs about the universal combining of God and nature caused his excommunication and humiliation. Only centuries later have his brilliant philosophical treaties been restored to their proper place in history.

Albert Einstein (1879–1955), a theoretical physicist, was born in Ulm, Germany, and died in Princeton, New York. He was the father of the theory of relativity. It pays to mention that during the years we spent in the DP camp in Ulm, there was neither mention nor a sign commemorating his being a native son.

A great void has been created between the Orthodox sects and secular Jews through alienation and hostility toward one another. The Orthodox ranks claim that the secular Jews just don't fit into their framework of religious *Yiddishkayt* (Judaism), and the secular Jews claim that the Orthodoxy is rigid and inflexible. Case in point, Jewish education, both Orthodox and secular, was once considered our crowning glory, and now Jewish education is on the periphery of Jewish existence.

Both the Orthodoxy and the secular Jews have blocked out the fact that, in the former Jewish life in Eastern Europe, be it in the big cities, *shtetlekh* (little towns), or villages, Jews of all religious, political, and social convictions lived alongside each other in almost

The Author teaching at Sholem Aleichem Folkshul #21 (Son Avi, 2nd from left)

perfect harmony, and in spite of their disagreements and different affiliations, both suffered the same fate during the Holocaust. To the Jew-hating slayers, we were all the same.

Jewish amnesia set in within several decades, striking the American continent as well as and including, to our consternation, the Jewish State of Israel. Today, most of the Israeli Jews, Sephardim as well as Ashkenazim, are orphaned of both their cultural and historical past. The Sephardim, Jews of Spanish and Middle Eastern heritage, have almost lost their culture altogether. It was Professor Dov Noy, the well-known Israeli-American folklorist and scholar, who promulgated this fact in his lectures and writings both in Israel and in the United States, lamenting the great loss of both Ashkenazi and Sephardic cultures.

I would like to share with you the fact that I personally am not a religious Jew, but every semester, in order to expose my Columbia University Yiddish language students to the breath and width of Jewish identity, I took them to a little town in Upstate New York

The Author teaching at Sholem Aleichem Folkshul #21

called Kiryas Yoel (named for the Satmar Rabbi Yoel Teitelbaum of the Satmar Jewish sect and known for its extreme view of Judaism). The village men, women, and children all speak Yiddish, albeit quite Anglicized. My aim was to show my students an image of a *shtetl* (little town). This village's version of a *shtetl* never actually existed in Eastern Europe; it was merely a concocted version of a rabbi's vision of a *shtetl,* maybe even his own. It pays to add that, in an actual Eastern European Yiddish *shtetl,* Jews lived side by side with their Jewish neighbors. The Jews were Orthodox and secular, their offspring sometimes chose to be affiliated with Zionist, Communist, Bundist, and Anarchist movements. Jews also lived side by side with their non-Jewish neighbors. Their relationship depended strictly on the conditions of their Christian governing bodies and political circumstances. There were plenty of pogroms to go around.

Yearly, before Passover, I would take my students to a *Matze* (matzah) factory in Brooklyn, where we witnessed how *Shmure Matze* (guarded matzah) is baked. It was quite expensive and eaten in Jewish Orthodox homes or brought as a gift to good friends for Passover.

We also visited an inspection center for *Mezuzas* (door amulets) and *Tfiln* (phylactery boxes worn by religious men on their forehead and left arm). We were enlightened by the young men and learned that they mostly dealt with cases of dreadful events that sometimes befell an Orthodox Jewish household. If such an event occurred, the first thing to be done was to inspect the *Mezuze,* to see whether any letters in the inspected prayers were damaged so they could be either corrected or replaced. We also visited a *Mikveh* (ritual bath) for Orthodox women, who are obliged to immerse themselves after their monthly menstrual period. The men and boys had a separate *Mikveh.*

All through the semester, I would take my students to the National Yiddish Theater, the *Folksbiene,* as well as to the YIVO Institute for Jewish Research and the *Jewish Forward Newspaper,* and organized Yiddish Theatrical events on campus with two famous Yiddish actresses, Mina Bern and Reyzl Bozhik, performing their repertoire.

On campus, we celebrated a "Mock Jewish Wedding" with a fake student-bride and groom, along with their mock Jewish in-laws. The mock ceremony was performed by the Columbia University Chabad rabbi. A band played Yiddish wedding music and dances, and kosher food was served according to Jewish dietary laws and customs.

Aside from my many classes on subjects ranging from literature to film to theatre and humor, it was my duty to expose my students to as many Jewish and Yiddish cultural experiences as possible. When I began teaching Yiddish at Columbia University in 1990, I had four students in one beginner's class. By the time I retired in 2015, my classes consisted of eighty students.

The Author (2nd from left) teaching at Columbia University, 2015

In Conclusion

The world has not changed. As I look around today, I see the same brutality and inhumanity that I describe in this book continue. The news from Putin's Russia seems eerily consistent with my tales of Stalin's Soviet Union. The slave labor camps of North Korea are still functioning to enslave innocent victims just as the Siberian Gulag did in my lifetime. The crematorium in modern-day Syria performs the same function as Hitler's multitude of gas chambers and their accompanying furnaces. Anti-Semitism, hatred, prejudice, and extremism are still prevalent and the world remains silent.

As I conclude the writing of this book, it crosses my mind that the letter we received from the Kremlin so many years ago granting us our new abode came with rigid instructions to go directly to the new police station, show the Kremlin-letter to the officer who kept the registry of all residents in our new district and provide him with all of our personal information in order to be registered as tenants in our new region.

When my mother and I stayed with a family in the city of Lwow (Lemberg, today Lwiw), waiting for my father to join us in our escape, the lady of the house warned us that the authorities were searching for nonregistered residents and stated that we must leave immediately.

With the reports of Russia's purported interference in the U.S. election and the recent proposal to register U.S. citizens with the federal authorities—our individual names, addresses, political party affiliation, social security numbers, and so on, a chill ran down my spine. I'm suddenly back to those days when I was a young refugee girl who escaped that oppression only to be reminded of how easily an advanced society can devolve. I am concerned that our free democracy should not fall into the Russian trap.

I have been an educator all my life, and I leave you with this question: When will we ever learn?

The Author teaching at Columbia University

Acknowledgments

First and foremost I owe my gratitude to my father, Chaim Schmule-witz, who encouraged me to write from an early age.

My husband, Mendl Hoffman, who guided me through my higher education, delighted in my writing ability, and stood by me in moments of doubt.

My son Avrum (Avi) Hoffman, who painstakingly put in hours of bringing this book to fruition.

My son Benyumin (Ben) Hoffman, who always stands by me in times of need.

My wonderful teacher, Chaim Kazhdan, at the Jewish Teacher's Seminary who inspired and instilled in me a great love for the Yiddish language, literature, and specifically to be enthralled, like he was, with the most beloved of Yiddish poets—Itzik Manger.

Avrum Sutzkever, one of our Shakespeares, most renowned Yiddish poet, for his friendship and encouragement, insisting I write not one, but two books simultaneously.

David Matis, Assistant Editor of the Jewish (Yiddish) Forward, who sneaked me into the newspaper as a columnist while the editor was away on vacation.

Professor Rakhmiel Peltz, former chairman of the Yiddish Program at Columbia University's Germanic Department, who believed in my educational skills and encouraged my participation in the search for a Yiddish lecturer.

Rena Berkowitz-Borow, my sidekick and cowriter of several plays.

Joseph Papp aka Yosele Papirowsky, world-famous impresario and Founder of NY Shakespeare Festival/Public Theater as well as Free Shakespeare in the Park, who delighted in the Yiddish language and was the first to produce "Songs of Paradise," at the Public Theater.

Beverly Koenigsberg, who helped translate a number of my short stories.

Aviva Astrinsky, close friend and former chief librarian at Yivo Institute for Jewish Research for her help in my research.

Feigele (Florence) Edelstein, my childhood friend who is always there to assist me in times of need.

Dr. Dovid Katz, the most brilliant Yiddish linguist to date, who invited me to participate in several teaching assignments at Oxford University in England, and at the University of Vilnius in Lithuania.

Sam Norich, former executive director of Yivo, now president of the Forward and executive director of the Forward Association. He was the first to associate the Yivo with the Joseph Papp Yiddish Theater.

The good-hearted William (Bill) Dellinger, office manager at the Germanic Department at Columbia University, always ready to be of great help.

Peggy Quinsenberry, secretary in the Germanic Department of Columbia University, full of kindness and assistance.

Krayndl (Cornelia) Martyn, one of my best students at Columbia University who became a Yiddish professor herself at the University of Potsdam in Germany.

Judy Slater, for her first read and edit of the book.

Carol and Gary Rosenberg (The Book Couple) for their help in making this book a reality.

About the Author

Miriam Hoffman earned her first baccalaureate (B.A.) in 1957 from the Jewish Teachers Seminary in New York, which was accepted at the New School for Social Research in New York in 1981, upon her return from a decade living in Israel. In 1982, she earned her second B.A. at the University of Miami.

In 1982, Miriam was accepted at Columbia University of New York and majored in Yiddish folklore and literature, where she did all her graduate work. Today she is Professor of Yiddish language, literature, Jewish culture, Yiddish humor, classical and minor Yiddish writers, and a course called 20th Century Yiddish Literature and Film. She taught at Columbia University from 1992 to 2015.

Miriam has also written a Yiddish textbook called *Key to Yiddish*, which includes scholarly research, conversation, folklore, folktales, songs, and literary works by the most acclaimed Yiddish writers and poets. *Key to Yiddish* also contains humorous illustrations that appeared in the Yiddish magazine *Der Groyser Kundas,* in print from 1911 to 1929. *Key to Yiddish* contains close to 700 pages.

The very last chapter in *Key to Yiddish* includes Miriam's

successful play called *The Maiden of Ludmir,* which deals with the first female Orthodox rabbi in the Ukraine of 1805–1892. *The Maiden of Ludmir* was performed at the Folksbiene Theater. *Key to Yiddish* is now used in many universities all over the world.

Miriam is also a successful Yiddish playwright. She has written many plays as *Reflections of a Lost Poet,* which deals with the life and works of the most beloved Yiddish poet Itzik Manger and which is still being performed today both in the United States, in Israel and, as of 2016, is being staged in Bucharest, Romania.

Miriam has written several plays with Rena Borow, among them the play *Noble Laureate.* Isaac Bashevis-Singer was the Nobel Laureate for Literature in 1978, and the play is named after a since-corrected misspelling on his tombstone. The play tells of Isaac Bashevis-Singer's battle with dementia in the declining years of his

The Author Graduating Workmen's Circle Mitlshul (2nd row, 1st from left)

191

life in Miami Beach, Florida. It was performed at the Queens Theater in the Park in New York City.

Miriam's plays were also staged at the Folksbiene National Yiddish Theater of New York, The Yiddish Theatre of Saidye Bronfman, the Centre for the Arts in Montreal, Canada, and the Yiddishpiel Theater in Israel. Miriam is the recipient of the Israeli Tony Award for her Yiddish translation of Neil Simon's *The Sunshine Boys.* Her Yiddish translation of Mel Brooks's *The Producers* was performed to great acclaim in 2016. It ran for several months to sold-out houses at the Dora Wasserman Yiddish Theater and the Alvin Siegel Center in Montreal, Canada.

Miriam is also a known Yiddish journalist and worked as a feature writer for the *Yiddish Forward* from 1982 to today.

The years 2014–2015 saw Miriam's retirement from Columbia University after twenty-five years of dedicated work. Since then, she is still busy writing her column for the *Yiddish Forward,* and working on a new Yiddish play called *Shiklgruber and Dzugashvili,* the original names of Hitler and Stalin, a musical comedy in two acts. Miriam still lectures on the topic of "Yiddish in Living Color."

The Author's AEF DP Registration Record
(from International Tracing Service, Bad Arolsen, Germany)